THE PROFESSOR'S NIGHTMARE (AND OTHER STORIES)

THREE ELI MARKS MYSTERY NOVELLAS

JOHN GASPARD

ALBERT'S BRIDGE
BOOKS

THE PROFESSOR'S NIGHTMARE

Three Eli Marks Mystery Novellas

First Edition | November 2023

www.elimarksmysteries.com

"The Square Circle" first appeared in a 2022/23 Prolific Works promotional program.

LOST IN THE SHUFFLE

Special thanks to Scott Wells.

Someone else is always going to grab it,
And someone else has always got the means.
And as long as it's up for sale, honey,
Your grass will never be that green.
And you get lost in the shuffle.

"Lost In The Shuffle"
Gary Rue & Leslie Ball

1

"Magic Camp is odd," I said. "It's a short phrase, yet I have issues with every syllable of it. I find the idea of spending a week focused on nothing but *magic* sort of appalling. And then there's the word *camp*, which suggests Work Camps, Prison Camps and Death Camps. My point is: why does this magic camp thing have to actually involve camping?"

Harry grunted at me, which was the first indication he'd given that he'd even been listening to my short but passionate tirade. As I had learned in my teens, Harry brought new meaning to the word cantankerous.

An early memory consisted of another, older magician (older than me, that is), confiding he was terrified of Harry. This admission was followed by one of the keenest descriptions of Harry ever uttered: "Your uncle could stare a bowl of oatmeal off the table."

He still possesses that power to this day. It may have even grown, exponentially.

Assured I was finished with my nominal diatribe, Harry looked up at me and slowly shook his head.

"In the first place, it can hardly be called *camping*. You'll have a cabin with your own room. Air conditioning. And indoor plumbing, for goodness' sake," he began. "Plus, three square meals a day in an equally-air-conditioned dining hall. So, you're hardly roughing it.

"And, in the second place," he continued quickly before I could insert a comment. "You were the one who signed up for it. I don't recall anyone holding a gun to your head. So quit your bellyaching."

"I have no idea why I ever agreed to do this," I said. Although I'd never admit it, the whine in my voice was beginning to annoy even me.

"I believe it had something to do with weeks of below-zero temperatures and a windchill factor that was practically comic in its intensity," Harry offered. "At the time you were near giddy with the notion of spending warm days sunning your pasty, pale form on a bucolic lakeside."

"That's just the sales hype. In truth, I'll be stuck in cramped, humid cabins with sweaty, gangly teenagers, watching them execute tragic double lifts and excruciatingly awful second deals," I said. "Not to mention drowning in a sea of Rubik's cubes."

"You're being well paid, and you'll have the satisfaction of mentoring the next generation of magicians."

"If it's so great, why aren't you doing it?"

"Because I'm not an idiot," Harry said, neatly bringing our discussion to a close.

* * *

"Are you sure you've packed enough stuff?" This was said sarcastically by my lovely wife. At least, it sounded sarcastic.

Ignoring her tone, I surveyed the three suitcases and the duffle bag. "On the contrary, I think I've gone rather lean in my approach to packing," I said, as I added the duffle to the other cases in the back of the car. I closed the hatchback and gave it an extra shove, to make sure the ancient lock had indeed latched. "This is your last chance to join me."

Megan shook her head. "A week in the middle of nowhere with hormone hopped-up teens who are also magicians? Don Draper himself couldn't put a positive spin on that nightmare scenario." She smiled up at me. "But I'm sure *you'll* have a great time."

"I still don't understand why this all can't take place at a hotel," I whined as I pushed on the hatch one last time. I don't know why, but I have never trusted that hatch lock.

"Maybe because Magic Hotel doesn't sound nearly as rustic as Magic Camp," Megan suggested. "Do you have water for the car?"

Megan had switched effortlessly out of sarcastic spouse mode and into her more natural caring wife attitude.

I nodded. "My hydration needs are covered, no problem." I had filled three water bottles and had a thermos full of coffee, all within easy reach on the front seat.

"Call me when you get there."

"I've heard that cell service is spotty, but I'll do my best."

She gave me a quick peck on the cheek. "Have fun."

I opened the driver's door and turned back. "Last chance for a week at magic camp."

"Not on your life," she said with a smile.

Although neither of us knew it at the time, more prescient words have rarely been spoken.

* * *

MANY MINNESOTA TOURISTS, when traveling north on Highway 35, make a point of taking a pitstop in Hinkley, Minnesota. The town is famous for two things: A big, town-leveling fire, and the sweet rolls (of the caramel and cinnamon variety) at Tobie's Restaurant and Bakery. The fire took place in the late 1800s, but the rolls are created daily. And they are legendary. Although, in my case, essentially mythical. Because I've never tasted them.

Ever the contrarian, my uncle Harry had always made a point of zooming past Hinkley (exit 183) whenever we were headed that way (to Duluth or other northernly destinations). While many cars slowed to leave the freeway—destined for what I was convinced must be the greatest sweet rolls known to man—Harry would speed up, headed toward his own utopian destination.

Moose Lake. And the Moose Lake Cafe.

"Best sweet rolls in the world," Harry would say with a grin as he hit the accelerator. "Beats those doughy monstrosities at Tobie's by a country mile."

All these years later—even though I was on my own and free of his avuncular strictures—I too sped past exit 183. Fifteen minutes later, I found myself pulling into the barely paved parking lot for the Moose Lake Cafe.

I found a spot between two massive potholes and turned off the ignition. Although I had no point of comparison, I knew Harry was correct on at least one point: the Moose Lake Cafe did produce a stunning (some might say World Class) variety of sweet rolls.

And that was why I had stopped. Well, to be honest, the thermos full of coffee I'd consumed also offered strong inspiration. I had been on the road for two hours and still had at least another three and a half hours ahead of me. So, a bathroom break and a seat at the counter for a quick snack seemed like a fine idea.

I ordered a caramel roll and another cup of coffee, adding more unnecessary caffeine to my already overloaded system. The roll, when it came, was large and gooey and still warm. The first bite sent a sugar jolt throughout my central nervous system that challenged, if only for a moment, the caffeine buzz which was currently holding sway.

"I feel silly eating a sweet roll with a knife and fork, but I don't see any other option," said a voice.

I turned to see a burly man perched on the stool next to me. He was about halfway through his own bakery selection, which appeared to be an imposing cinnamon roll. The dainty manner in which he handled the cutlery was in strong contrast with his bulk and hulking demeanor. I don't want to trade in stereotypes, but the odds of him being a trucker—as opposed to, say, an accountant—seemed strong.

"Mmmm," I replied, my mouth still full of my most recent, over-sized bite.

"Headed north?"

I nodded.

"Vacation?"

I shrugged, still chewing.

"Work?"

I nodded, finally getting the mass of pastry under control in my mouth.

"What do you do?"

Ah, the dreaded question.

The honest answer would be to say 'magician,' but I hesitated. This was my natural reaction to that question, a response which I have never fully understood. It was probably because my truthful answer had, on more than one occasion, been followed up by an annoying additional question: 'No, no, I mean what's your real job?'

Real job indeed.

I'd only had the one job so far in my life and have done just fine by it, thank you very much. Over the years, I'd bought two new cars, put down half the deposit on a house, paid the full cost of moving out of that house, and covered my share of two weddings and a divorce (not in that order, of course).

In fairness, though, that second wedding had been purchased with a BOGO coupon. But regardless, I was doing just fine. Nothing to be ashamed of.

In the past, I had often just said "Consultant," as that answer was usually sufficiently boring enough to stifle any further conversational explorations.

I recognized, of course, that this impulsive denial was perfectly in keeping with my current mood toward the art and craft of magic. For the last few months, I'd found I wasn't enjoying performing the way I had in the past. I wasn't finding any bubbly excitement at the discovery of new tricks. And to be honest, the company of other magicians had on more than one occasion put my teeth on edge.

A quote by the wonderful magician, Eugene Burger, had been bouncing around in my head for the last few months: "Everyone wants to change, but no one wants to do anything differently."

He also had famously said, "All magic is about trans-formation."

I couldn't quite put my finger on it, but somehow, Eugene had quite neatly diagnosed my emotional condition. I was living somewhere between those two quotes.

Yet, in spite of it all, I was on my way to spend a week with thirty or so budding magicians. The logic of that choice was still eluding me as I looked over at the large man, who was patiently waiting for an answer to what was—in most situa-tions—a pretty straight-forward question.

"I'm a magician," I finally said.

Mercifully, he didn't follow this confession with the afore-mentioned "What's your real job?" Or the other threadbare classic, "Great, can you make my wife disappear?"

Instead, he surprised me with this: "Huh. I used to be a magician. I kinda miss it."

He returned his attention back to his cinnamon roll, and I

took another Heimlich-inducing forkful of my own caramel monstrosity. For some reason, though, I couldn't let his remark just hang there in the air, unanswered.

"Used to be?" I began, once my chewing had subsided. "Why did you quit?"

He shrugged. "I grew up," he finally said.

I was immediately reminded of a story my uncle Harry used to tell about his friend, magician Jay Marshall. A kid came up to him after a show and said, "When I grow up, I want to be a magician." To which Jay Marshall (allegedly) replied, "Son, you can't do both."

"You headed to a gig?"

I nodded. "Sort of. A week at Magic Camp."

He smiled wistfully. "Magic Camp. Always wanted to go. Never could. Sounds like fun."

I shrugged. "The jury's out on that one. So, what did you used to do? Cards? Coins? Mentalism?"

"Oh, I was a card guy. Nothing too fancy, not a lot of knacky stuff, none of those knuckle busters. Just straight forward, mind-bending stuff. My favorite was by Max Maven. B'Wave. Not sure if you know it, it's a short, really clever version of the Brainwave deck."

I reached for my wallet and he must have thought I was headed out.

"Well, anyway, nice to meet you," he began, but I waved it away. I pulled four playing cards from my wallet and laid them on the counter between us.

"B'Wave," I said as I gestured toward the cards. "I never leave home without it."

He stared at the cards and then glanced at me, clearly asking for permission to touch them. I nodded and he picked them up slowly, almost lovingly, as he sorted through the four cards.

"Oh boy, did I love this trick," he finally said. "Of course, like most teenage magicians, I quickly ran out of audiences to do it for."

"A common problem," I agreed.

"But I still remember watching the video of Max Maven demonstrating the trick, and the little subtleties he offered. You've seen the video, right?"

I shook my head. "I'm a little ashamed to admit this, but I actually learned the trick from Max, when he came through town," I said.

"Lecture tour?"

"No, he was visiting a friend. My uncle," I confessed.

"Nothing to be ashamed of there," the man agreed.

"It gets worse," I continued. "The best subtleties I learned for the trick actually came from a conversation I had with Eugene Burger."

"Okay, now I officially hate you," he said.

"That's okay, I would hate me too," I agreed. "Those guys were all friends of my Uncle Harry."

He tilted his large head to one side and squinted at me.

"Not Harry Marks, by any chance?"

"One in the same," I admitted.

"Wow. You know, one of the first magic books I ever got was his. The one with all the tricks and the dumb jokes. Although they didn't seem dumb at the time."

"*Harry's Magic Emporium.*"

"That's the one. And he's your uncle?"

"Guilty as charged."

"I'm Chad, by the way," he said, extending a beefy hand in my direction.

"Eli," I offered as I watched my hand disappear into his.

He pulled his hand back and glanced at his watch. "Look, I don't have to be back on the road for a while. Any chance you want to hang out and talk about magic for a few minutes?"

It would have been an easy offer to turn down, as I was on a schedule, albeit not a tight one. However, his nature was so pleasant and about as far away from the hormonal teenage magician bath I was about to step into, that I found myself quickly agreeing.

With a nod to the waitress behind the counter, we gathered our cups and the remains of our rolls and moved across the small cafe to one of many empty booths.

IN MAGICIAN PARLANCE, what we did for the next hour is usually called "sessioning." I'm really not sure why that term came into fashion, but it's the one everyone uses. In general, it means sitting around with a small group of magicians, showing off tricks and discussing moves. Or just showing off.

In my early years, I had spent countless days (and nights) at magic conventions, sitting with other magicians in the lobby, "sessioning" for hours on end.

At the time, I couldn't wait for these sessions.

Nowadays, in those rare instances when I attend a convention, I'm usually in bed and asleep long before any real sessioning begins.

As soon as we sat down, I pulled out a deck of cards and put them on the table between us.

"You always carry a deck?" Chad asked with a grin.

"More often than not," I admitted. "Force of habit."

I'd come to realize that, in the magic world, there are really just two types of magicians: performers who always have a trick or two on their person and are willing to perform at the drop of a hat; and performers who take great umbrage at being asked to perform outside of their traditional stage environment.

I had, in my own unique manner, become a hybrid of those two types: I always carried a deck of cards. And I was always deeply annoyed when someone asked me to use them.

Chad picked up the box and slid the cards out, getting a feel for the deck.

"Been a while since I did this," he said as he glanced over at me. "Got any favorite moves?"

That was an open-ended question if I'd ever heard one, and for the next few minutes we traded stories and swapped trick versions. I showed him my Ambitious Dog routine (with apologies to David Regal). Chad wowed me with a well-executed second-deal poker hand, which left him with four aces and me with nothing to write home about.

"You've still got some chops," I said as he gathered the cards and gave them a quick shuffle.

"They say it's like riding a bike," he agreed. "But then, they say a lot of stupid stuff."

"Sorry if it feels like I've been ignoring you two," came a harried voice. It was our waitress, stopping by to refill our nearly full coffee cups. Her nametag said Ruby. "We're a little short-handed today."

"No problem," I said. "Sorry we've hogged this booth for so long."

"Not to worry," Ruby said. "The other girl—Darlene— called in sick. Or so she alleged. Hungover or heartbroken, take your pick. As a result, I've been running around like a head with its chicken cut off. Thankfully, things have finally started to calm down."

She glanced around the cafe and I followed her gaze: Although the place had been nearly full when I'd arrived (hence the need to sit at the counter), there were now only about a dozen or so customers.

"I guess the rush has passed," I agreed.

"Mercifully," she said as she added a few unnecessary drops to each of our coffee cups. "You fellas playing cards?"

"No, just doing a couple card tricks," Chad said as he absently executed a pretty clean one-handed shuffle.

"Really? Can you show me one?" Ruby seemed to suddenly perk up at the prospect of a distraction (<u>any</u> distraction) from her other duties.

I was glad the cards were in Chad's hands, which meant the onus to respond to her request—either positively or negatively —fell to him.

"Sure thing," Chad said.

I watched his face and could practically read his mind: He was quickly calculating what trick he could successfully retrieve from his long-disused repertoire that would work in this impromptu situation. A flash of an idea crossed his face. He quickly spread the cards and held them out toward the waitress.

"Pick a card," he said with a wide grin.

Although I didn't know the details, I recognized—from long experience—where this was headed. So, I took the opportunity to excuse myself to make a quick trip to the Mens Room. A glance around the sparsely populated cafe helped me locate the RESTROOMS sign. And, once I got there, it only took me a moment longer to decipher the two cute labeling options the restaurant had landed on (Bucks and Does).

A couple minutes later, I exited the restroom and was about to head back to my booth—hoping against hope the card trick had reached its inevitable conclusion.

But I stopped in mid-step.

Although I'd been gone for a very brief time, the small cafe now appeared to be completely empty. All the patrons had vaporized.

In fact, only one person now occupied the space.

He was standing in the middle of the room.

He looked—not to put too fine a point on it—a bit crazed.

And he was holding a gun.

2

Of course, it only took a moment for me to realize the cafe hadn't lost all its customers. On the contrary, everyone who had been there when I headed to the bathroom was still there.

But now they were all lying—awkwardly and nervously—on the floor.

I'm not sure what this large-scale change in position meant, but my gut told me it wasn't likely to be a positive thing. My fight or flight instinct (such as it is), kicked in.

As usual, I opted immediately for flight.

I quietly stepped backward. At the same moment, I instinctively patted my pocket for my phone.

It wasn't there.

A glance across the dining room confirmed my dim memory: I could see the phone right where I had left it, on the table. It rested comfortably next to the paltry remains of my cinnamon roll.

If using my phone to call for help had been Plan A, my mind reeled to quickly develop an operational Plan B. I scanned my short-term memory: had there been a window in the Mens Room?

There had not.

Okay, what other exit options were available?

The guy with the gun was standing between me and the front door. So that wasn't a likely candidate for a speedy exit.

Was there an exit out of the cafe other than the front door? There had to be. I mean, wasn't there a law or something?

I glanced around the room without seeing any obvious forms of egress. If there was another exit, in order to access it, I'd have to go through the kitchen. And to go through the kitchen, I'd have to step over the trembling body of the short order cook who was currently prone on the floor. He was halfway in the kitchen and halfway in the dining room.

I was beginning to accept the grim realization of just how few options I had.

"I tell you, Jimmy, Darlene isn't here," came the voice of our waitress, Ruby.

From my odd vantage point, I could only see her worn and scuffed orthopedic shoes; the rest of her was obscured by the counter. She was on the floor, by our booth. Chad was next to her, his bulky form not really built for floor exercises such as this.

He caught my eye. The large man looked scared. Terrified, even.

I imagine he was identifying a similar look on my face.

"Well, she's not at home and she's not at her mother's," said the gunmen. I assumed he must be Jimmy. "So that leaves here at the diner. I need to talk to her."

"I'm sure you do, darling," Ruby said, a nervous tremble obvious in her voice. "Why don't you let me give her a call and we'll straighten this all out."

"She's not answering my calls, what makes you think she'll answer yours?"

The tone with which he uttered this statement offered a myriad of reasons why Darlene—or any sane person—might prefer to let Jimmy's calls go into voicemail.

Ruby didn't have an answer to his question. The silence of her non-response hung heavy in the air. We were all frozen, not sure what to do—or not to do—in this situation.

That's why, to this day, I don't know why I then said what I said.

"Perhaps she'll take my call," I offered.

Jimmy spun at the sound of my voice. It may have been a trick of the light, but it appeared like his gun spun faster than he did.

"Who are you and why aren't you on the floor with everyone else?"

Those were two excellent questions. My mind swirled as I attempted to form an answer to either one of them.

"I'm a guy who was in the bathroom," I said slowly. "So, I guess I missed the first act of this drama. As to why Darlene might take my call," I continued, my mind in a literal tizzy as I searched for anything resembling an answer. "It might be because she doesn't know me. She has no preconceptions. A clean slate, as it were, vis-à-vis me. A tabula rasa, if you will."

Why I had picked this moment to mimic the vocal patterns of William F. Buckley, Jr., was a question for another day.

However, the concept of me placing the call seemed to register positively on the gunman's face. I'm not sure the idea actually made any sense, but it must have clicked somewhere in Jimmy's brain. I noticed he lowered the gun; it was only nominally, maybe an inch. But it was a start.

"She does have a bad habit of picking up calls from Unknown Callers," Jimmy said slowly. "I tell her it's probably spam, somebody in a call center somewhere, or a computer. But that doesn't stop her from picking up."

"Well, I would certainly register as an Unknown Caller if I

called her from my phone," I said quickly. I then pointed
toward my phone on the table in the booth across the room. I'm
guessing this was to prove to Jimmy I had all the requirements
needed for placing a phone call to a stranger. "I could get her
on the phone and maybe we can straighten this out."

"She didn't say 'yes,'" Jimmy said quietly. I wasn't even sure
he had heard me. "I said, 'Darlene, will you marry me?' And
she didn't hesitate one second. She just turned and walked out
the door."

"Maybe she misunderstood the question," I suggested.
"Maybe that's what happened. Listen, I've been around tons of
marriage proposals. Sometimes, the ladies, you know, they get a
bit flustered."

I couldn't believe I had used the term 'the ladies,' but this
clearly wasn't the time to go back and re-state it. At least I'd
stopped talking like Buckley, which seemed like a step in the
right direction. Jimmy didn't appear to care; he had latched on
to something else in my last sentence.

"Why have you been around tons of marriage proposals?
Are you a minister or something?"

I wasn't really tracking with his logic on that one. I couldn't
think of many situations where someone would bring a
member of the clergy to a proposal. They were generally
reserved for a key role later in the bridal process. But this didn't
seem like the best time to pick nits.

"I'm a performer, a magician," I stammered. "A lot of times,
guys ask me to help them propose to their girlfriends."

I wasn't sure I was making myself understood; it might have
had something to do with the gun, which was pointed in my
general direction. I was afraid I was giving him the erroneous
impression that I roamed the country, helping young men in
their proposal aspirations. Like the Johnny Appleseed of
weddings. I felt some clarification was required.

"I mean, during my show," I continued. "As part of my magic act."

"And they say yes?" Jimmy asked. There was a dim note of hope in his raspy voice.

"Generally, yes, they do," I replied.

I didn't add, of course, that on more than one occasion, the bride-to-be had said 'yes' on-stage, but gave every indication she really meant 'no.' In these instances, I got the distinct impression her apparent jolly mood would shift the moment she got off stage.

Uncle Harry was always amused when I recounted these stories. "I admire the hutzpah of these fellows," he'd say. "Me, I'm like most trial attorneys: I would never ask a question unless I was darned sure in advance what they answer would be. But Godspeed to those brave fools."

Of course, I recognized my new friend, Jimmy, had already received what sounded like a definitive answer to his query. And I was pretty sure I didn't have it within my power to alter that outcome. However, I realized that I was—at the very least —taking Jimmy's mind off the gun in his hand, if only briefly. And that seemed like a good thing.

"Why don't I try to get Darlene on the phone and let's see if we can sort this thing out?" I suggested. I was doing my best to sound relaxed and casual about this plan. In truth, I felt just the opposite. But I must have done a good job of covering those anxieties, because suddenly Jimmy seemed pretty gung-ho about this proposal. Certainly, more than poor Darlene had been about the one he had proffered.

"Sure, let's do it. Make the call," he said. He waved the gun at me, and then pointed it toward my booth. I guess that meant I was okay to go pick up my phone.

As I slowly made my way across the restaurant, I made eye contact with several of the other customers, lying prone on the worn tile floor. Most looked afraid, which seemed like a

reasonable response to the situation. They all looked uncomfortable.

"You know, maybe you should let these folks go home while
we sort this out with Darlene on the phone," I said as I slowly
moved past Jimmy. "Some of them look pretty uncomfortable."

Jimmy shook his head vehemently. "No way. The second
any of these folks step out of here, they'll be on the phone to
the Sheriff. And that's another headache I just don't need this
morning."

I nodded agreeably. I considered suggesting that—sooner
or later—the Sheriff was clearly going to become deeply
involved in this situation. But I recognized that might be a
conversation for later.

"Well, at the very least, maybe they could all get up and sit
in chairs?" I offered.

"Nope," he said flatly. "It's safer for me—and for everyone—
if they stay on the floor."

I couldn't help but be reminded of an early lesson my Uncle
Harry had taught me about kids shows. He'd said that I should
make my young audience sit on the floor, and not in chairs,
during my presentation.

"Little ones have a natural tendency to want to rush the
stage," he'd advised after my first kids show had turned into
something of a free-for-all. "So, make them sit on the floor, not
in chairs. It's too easy to jump up out of a chair. Getting up from
a sitting position on the floor takes more time. And those extra
few seconds can mean the difference between a great show and
a disaster."

As always, Harry's advice had proven to be one hundred
percent correct. I recognized the same principle was at work in
this decidedly distinctive situation.

I continued to make my way across the room as another
thought hit me. I was only feet away from a man who was
pointing a gun in my general direction. And all I could think

about was a quote from a gangster movie. I wasn't sure who the actor was (it might have been Al Pacino), but I sort of remembered the advice he had offered the guys in his gang.

"You charge a guy who's got a gun. If he has a knife, you run away."

Was that what he'd advised? Or was it, "You charge a guy who's got a knife. If he has a gun, you run away"?

In this moment, they both made the same amount of sense to me.

I decided to—as they say—put a pin in that idea. For now.

I made it to my booth without incident. As I reached for my phone, I glanced down at Chad, who was sprawled uncomfortably next to the bench seat.

We gave each other a quick look. His expression seemed to say, *"Hey, if we hadn't stuck around performing stupid card tricks for the last hour, we'd both be long gone and on the road. Magic has once again ruined my life."*

I may have been mis-reading the look on Chad's face, but that certainly described my own current feelings.

I grabbed the phone and turned back to the antsy gunman.

"What's Darlene's number?"

I thought this was a pretty basic question. But Jimmy gave me the blankest of looks in response.

"Um, her number," he mumbled. "Man, I know I know it."

Of course, on a very human level, I understood how he felt. And a quick glance around the room confirmed the shared group response to his situation. Although the customers were still scared, many nodded at his predicament.

Nobody knows anyone's phone number by heart anymore.

While I could still recite the phone number from my childhood home with ease, I would be hard pressed to state—with any degree of accuracy—phone numbers for my wife, my uncle, and even the magic store I owned.

Jimmy struggled for several seconds to pull the number

from the recesses of his memory. And then he finally gave up. With a disgusted grunt, he shifted the gun from one hand to the other, then pulled his phone from his back pocket. After several annoyed swipes across its screen, he turned it toward me.

I slowly stepped forward, leaning in to see the number on the screen.

And I thought, "Charge at a knife, run from a gun? Or run from a knife, charge at a gun?"

Both—and neither—made sense to me. So, instead, I dutifully read the number off his screen as I dialed it into my phone.

I hit the button to make the call. For a second, I considered hitting the SPEAKER button. But a glance over at Jimmy's anxious expression convinced me the wisest move would be to skip that step.

I put the phone to my ear and listened as the phone rang on the other end.

I looked over at Jimmy and nodded reassuringly.

"It's ringing."

I turned my attention back to the phone. I wasn't sure what to do if she picked up. I was equally unclear as to my next best step if she didn't.

I was—as Uncle Harry always liked to say—metaphorically wedged between a rock and another rock.

And then I heard the familiar click of the phone being answered at the other end.

"Hello?" Her voice was understandably quizzical.

"Hi, may I speak to Darlene?" I asked, trying to sound both friendly and not like a phone robot.

"Speaking."

"Hi, Darlene. My name is Eli. You don't know me. But we do know someone in common. Jimmy—"

She cut me off before I could finish my sentence.

"What has that fool gone and done now?"

I glanced at Jimmy. The phone was pressed against my ear, and I was pretty sure he couldn't hear what was going on at the other end.

"Funny you should ask," I said. "We've got a little situation down here at the diner. With Jimmy and a bunch of other folks. And it would sure be a huge help if you could swing by. Like, as soon as possible."

There was a long pause on the other end of the phone. "Who are you again?"

"My name's Eli and I'm here with ... with Ruby and a bunch of other folks. And it would be great if you could just bop on over."

That was the first time in my life I had ever said 'bop on over.' I made a mental note to never do it again.

"We can explain it all when you get here," I added. "I promise."

There was a silent pause, followed by a long sigh.

"Fine," she said, her voice soaked with resignation. "I'll be there in ten minutes."

"Great," I said, the relief evident in my voice. Finally, something was going right. But she had already hung up. I turned to Jimmy, who was looking at me expectantly.

I put something on my face that was meant to represent a reassuring smile.

"She's on her way."

3

A s it turned out, Darlene was absolutely true to her word. She arrived ten minutes later.

However, it may have been the longest ten minutes of my life. And I'm sure the others in the cafe—the folks stretched out on the floor like a failed game of Twister—felt every inch of those six hundred seconds.

I glanced around, doing a quick check of my fellow hostages. Understandably, no one seemed happy with their current situation. But—on the plus side—no one seemed to be in obvious distress, either. Many of them were staring past where I stood, at the counter behind me.

I turned to see why their interest was drawn there: On the counter was a heap of cell phones of various shapes and sizes. Jimmy must have made everyone put their phones on the counter before taking their positions on the floor. Hence the longing looks from the floor crowd. I realized our shared addiction to our phones was really being put to the test in this situation. While I'm sure the majority wanted their devices in order to call for official help, I was betting there were more than a few who also wanted a quick chance to check their email.

I turned my attention back to our quasi-host.

Jimmy didn't strike me as the most patient person in a normal situation; while we waited for Darlene's arrival, he paced the floor like the cliché of an expectant father in a 60s TV sitcom. But without the reassuring laugh track.

I was feeling his pain. While I too wanted Darlene to make her appearance sooner rather than later, I really had no idea of what to do when she walked through the door.

She had apparently refused Jimmy's first proposal of marriage. And I didn't see anything in this current scenario that was likely to shift her outlook over to the 'You bet! Let's tie the knot!' column.

"A magician, huh?" Jimmy said suddenly.

I nodded. "Yep."

"And you can make a living doing that? Being a magician, I mean?"

"Most days."

He considered this for a long moment. "Darlene and I saw a magician once. In Vegas. First magician I ever saw. Live, I mean. It was included in the package," he added quickly. I suppose he didn't want me thinking they'd gone out of their way to see magic.

"How was he?" Although this hardly seemed like the right moment for it, I'm always curious about people's reactions to seeing live magic for the first time.

Jimmy shrugged. "He was okay. I liked him. Had some good jokes. Darlene said it seemed like he spent a lot of time standing next to his black curtain when he made stuff appear and disappear."

I nodded, having no trouble imagining the type of act they'd seen.

"Next time you go, I can suggest some better recommendations," I offered.

"Thanks," he said with a nod.

I realized this might be in the running for the strangest conversation I'd ever had.

We stood there, awkwardly, for several seconds.

"I think I did it wrong," Jimmy said finally.

"Excuse me?"

"When I proposed, I think I did it wrong," Jimmy repeated.

"How so?"

"We were in town, at The Tap. I'd had a few," he began. "Darlene was ticked off because she said I was paying too much attention to the waitress. I didn't like that. So, to get back at her, I told her if she wanted to fit into her swimsuit this summer, maybe she should keep her hands off my cheese fries. She got mad and got up to leave. But I realized she was my ride home. If she left, I'd have to hoof it. So, I grabbed her hand, got down on one knee, and asked her to marry me."

"You got down on one knee?"

"Well, I sorta stumbled when she tried to pull away. And I ended up on one knee. But it seemed to fit the moment, so I stayed down there."

"Okay."

"And she pulled her hand away, swore at me and stormed out. That was two days ago."

"So," I said as I replayed the scene in my head. "She actually never said 'no'?"

Jimmy considered this. "I guess not. She just swore at me and left." He pondered this new information. "That's right: she didn't really say no. So maybe I still have a chance?"

I nodded, but I wasn't convinced. But then I realized I wasn't the one who needed convincing. "You may still have a chance," I agreed. "Absolutely."

"So how does this work?" he asked. He seemed suddenly rejuvenated and upbeat about where things might be headed with his reluctant fiancé.

I had been mulling that same question with little to show

for it. In a typical scenario, the guy would approach me before the show with his request. I'd then finagle a reason to get them both on-stage as volunteers for a trick. If I'd had enough advance notice, I could do a special trick, like *The Anniversary Waltz*. At the conclusion of that illusion, the boyfriend could then naturally segue into his proposal.

However, in this particular instance—as I was painfully aware—I had not been given any advance notice.

I certainly might have had what I needed to do *The Anniversary Waltz* in my car. But I didn't think Jimmy would be willing to authorize that short field trip. He wouldn't let me go out there on my own. And he certainly wouldn't accompany me, leaving his hostages unattended.

So as heartwarming as *The Anniversary Waltz* was, it wasn't going to be on the set list for this morning's performance.

Before I could head down a longer path of possible options, the eerie quiet of the cafe was shattered by a pounding on the door. This was followed by a voice which easily could have been used by the CIA as an illegal interrogation method.

"Jimmy, you idiot," came the sound from the other side of the door. "What stupid mess have you gotten yourself into this time?"

Jimmy turned to me and said the most obvious—and yet also somehow the most chilling—thing I'd heard all day.

"Darlene's here."

4
_____

J immy quickly trotted over to the cafe's front door, flipping
the deadbolt and pulling the door open. He dramatically
gestured for Darlene to enter.

She cautiously stepped into the room, quickly assessing the
situation. She was maybe an inch taller than Jimmy, but the
mound of hair piled on top of her head made her look even
taller. She pointed one long thin finger at the people on the
floor, sweeping her hand as she recognized faces. I could see
her nails were exceptionally long and individually painted.
They shimmered with glitter.

I was reminded of an old saying Uncle Harry had uttered
years before, about a cash register saleswoman who had barged
her way into the magic store: "Big hair, big nails, big trouble,"
he had mumbled. And he hadn't been far off.

"What are all these people doing on the floor, Jimmy? And
why was that front door locked? Do you see that sign?"

Jimmy—who was just re-locking the door—ducked as she
swung her arm past his head. I was surprised her primary
interest seemed to be the locked front door. And not the dozen
or so people sprawled on the floor.

"'This door must remain unlocked during business hours,'" Darlene read slowly, as if to a child. "Do you know what kind of trouble you can get us into if you lock that door during business hours?"

Given Jimmy's current compendium of transgressions, I didn't think his locking of the door would loom large on his list of crimes.

"I dunno," he mumbled.

"Unlock that door this second," Darlene snapped. "That's all this restaurant needs is another citation."

I was tempted to ask what the earlier citation had concerned, but Darlene was barreling forward. Once Jimmy had dutifully unlocked the door, she was again in his face.

"And what in the Sam Hill is Ruby doing on the floor? Ruby, get up. Get up right now."

Ruby gave her co-worker a weak smile. "I'd love to, hon. But Jimmy told us to lie down on the floor. And since he was swinging that gun around, it felt like maybe it would be best if I complied."

"Gun? What gun?" Darlene turned, her attention once again focused on Jimmy. She glanced down at his hand. Jimmy held up the gun, to prove that Ruby had been telling the truth. Darlene clucked her tongue and shook her head slowly from side to side. "Oh, Jimmy, what shenanigans have you gotten yourself into this time?"

"I did something wrong and I'm going to make it right," he said, clearly trying to put a note of defiance into this voice.

"What could you possibly make right by taking a dozen poor people hostage and making them lie down on this filthy floor."

I momentarily wondered if that earlier citation had been focused on overall cleanliness. But that fear was quickly superseded as I heard what Jimmy said next:

"Eli here is a magician and he's got something to say to you."

Darlene turned toward me, a look of accusation on her face.

"Oh, does he," she said. "Are you the fool who talked Jimmy into this twisted scenario?"

"No ma'am," I said quickly. "I'm one of the hostages."

"Are you now? Then why aren't you on the floor?"

"I was in the bathroom."

"Then why aren't you lying on the floor in the bathroom?"

"That's a very good question," I was forced to admit. "I guess because I didn't hear about the floor requirement until I got out here."

"I see." She gave me another long look. "So, Eli who is a magician. What was it you wanted to say to me?"

"I just had a few thoughts about couples and relationships," I said, segueing directly into my scripted introduction for *The Anniversary Waltz*. (A trick I knew full well I was not able to perform in this situation. But I soldiered on.) "What does it mean when we say we've found 'The One?' Just exactly what does that mean?"

Darlene gave me a long, icy stare. "I have no earthly idea."

"For some, it means that the universe has linked two people who were meant to be together," I continued. "So, tell me this: was it by mere chance—or was it actually fate—that brought you and Jimmy together?"

"The little bug has been pestering me since the ninth grade. His locker was just down the row from mine. Eventually I said, 'Oh, what the hell,' and gave in."

Her response was not what I usually got back in this situation. The patter for the routine was flexible, but not <u>that</u> flexible. I decided to wing it. The fact was, I couldn't do *The Anniversary Waltz*, and reciting the script for the trick wasn't going to make it so.

I heard Uncle Harry's voice in my head: "Go back to the basic principle: What is the effect you're trying to achieve?"

He had first asked this question of me when I was a fledgling magician who thought I knew more than I actually did. I had approached Harry proudly with a card trick I'd developed. He patiently watched me perform it. When I was done, he nodded and said, "Not bad, not bad. Do you mind if I futz with it?"

An hour later he came back and performed the same trick for me.

"Nice job," I said when he'd successfully completed it.

"Thanks," Harry said as he slid the cards back into their box. "I believe your version had six sleights. I got it down to just one pinkie break."

He looked up and must have seen the astonished look on my face. "Eli, how a trick is performed—all the sleights and that nonsense—is only of interest to other magicians. For the audience, you have to ask: What is the trick saying? What feeling does the effect evoke? The rest is just advertising."

As I'd come to learn, Harry was once again absolutely correct. And this was an idea I'd tried to take to heart ever since then.

So, what was the feeling *The Anniversary Waltz* evoked in the viewer? I think it was that the couple was fated to be together. It was literally in the cards.

I then flashed back to a wedding I'd gone to with my first wife, Deirdre. At the reception, the hired magician had approached our table. For some reason, he picked the two of us and proceeded to do a card trick—which he claimed—would prove we were meant to be together.

(I think the infallibility of the trick's assertion was seriously in doubt, as two months later Deidre served me with divorce papers.)

I had expected this wedding magician to do *The Anniversary*

Waltz, but instead he did a version of an *Any Card At Any Number* effect, in which the random number Deirdre had picked turned out to be the location for the card I had signed with her name.

Later that evening I tracked him down as he was packing up to leave and got the background on the routine. It was one which he had adapted from a trick in Barrie Richardson's *Theater of the Mind* book.

Standing in the middle of the cafe, I quickly tried to run through the phases of that routine, hoping I was remembering all of them. And in the right order.

I looked up. Darlene was staring at me blankly. I think my trip down memory lane had gone on longer than I'd realized.

"I think sometimes the universe is telling us we need to be together as a couple. We're fated to be together. And all we need to do is be open to what the universe is saying."

I looked over at Jimmy, who nodded at me appreciatively.

"Mind if I get my playing cards?" I gestured toward the booth across the room.

"Sure thing. Go for it. This is great," he said. He appeared to have more faith in the power of the trick—and in me—than I currently possessed.

I crossed the room to the booth I had been sharing with the truck driver. It seemed like a long time ago. Ruby and Chad were both still lying on the floor in front of the booth. I reached over Chad to grab the deck of cards off the table. As I did, I glanced down at the large man.

"What are you thinking of doing?" he asked quietly. "I'm guessing *The Anniversary Waltz* isn't an option."

"You're right on that," I said as I grabbed the deck of cards.

"I'd recommend *The Four Burglars,*" he said with a wink.

"*The Four Burglars,*" I repeated slowly. I hadn't thought of that trick in years.

I'd seen that card trick when I attended my first magic

convention as a teenager. While the trick had been impressive —four criminal Jacks distributed throughout the deck suddenly and magically appear back on the top of the deck—I was more impressed by the magician who performed it. If he was older than eight, I would have been surprised. And he did the trick really, really well. Far better than I could have at that time, and I easily had five or six years on him.

It was then I realized for the first—but not the last—time that, regardless of how good I got in magic, I would always be behind someone. There would always be people who knew more than I did; often, <u>a lot</u> more.

"That's why judging yourself against others is always an imperfect metric," Harry told me at the time. And again many times after.

"*The Four Burglars*," I repeated to Chad. "It's been years since I thought of that trick."

"Well, there's an obvious connection to being part of a criminal act. But for me, the ending can have the greatest impact," he said, again adding a wink. I was beginning to think he might have a tic of some kind.

I shifted the deck of cards from one hand to the other. Chad's mention of that old trick had almost made me forget my original plan: To do a variation on *Any Card At Any Number* that had the same emotional impact as *The Anniversary Waltz*.

I gave the deck a quick shuffle as I crossed the cafe, headed back toward the gunman and his highly reluctant girlfriend.

If I had faced a tougher audience in my performance career, I couldn't remember when.

5

"Do you believe in fate?"

"I don't know and I don't care." Darlene said this without any trace of a smile.

I've had tough volunteers before, but if a cake had been available at that moment, I would have happily presented it to her. There have been many times when I picked the absolute worst volunteer to invite on stage. I had improved my selection abilities over the years, but I still hit the occasional clunker.

But Darlene's complete indifference to the trick—and, apparently, to me—was in a league all its own.

"Well, as luck would have it, you don't have to believe in fate, because it's at work whether you believe in it or not." I said this with a too-big smile. I think I was trying to lessen Darlene's negativity by doubling down on my own positivity. "It's all, as they say, in the cards."

With that I gave the deck a showy shuffle and then spread the cards face up in front of the couple.

"Jimmy, look through these cards and pick the one that makes you think of Darlene," I said as I shifted the spread in his direction. "Just pick whichever card speaks to you."

He looked down at the well-mixed assortment and really studied them, like he was picking the best homemade cookie from a plate of options. It took him so long that I was tempted to repeat the instructions, thinking he may have become confused at some point. But before I had to resort to that, he pulled a card from the spread.

"The Queen of Hearts," he said with a broad grin as he held it up. Jimmy turned the card toward Darlene. "Because she is the queen of my heart."

"Ug," was Darlene's one syllable response.

I soldiered on.

"Fantastic," I said. I reached into my pocket and pulled out my ever-ready Sharpie marker. "Jimmy, why don't you sign your name across the face of that card?"

Jimmy did as instructed, writing his name slowly on the card, somehow balancing the gun in his hand as he did. He stared at the completed signature for what seemed like a long time. Finally, he looked back up at me.

I gave him my best reassuring smile as I took the card and placed it back into the deck. I began shuffling the cards as I continued with my hastily improvised spiel.

"So ... Jimmy has found his Queen and declared his love by writing his name on the card," I recounted. "And now that card has been lost in the shuffle, as they say. And so, this is where we turn to fate to decide the outcome."

I spread the cards in front of Darlene. This time they were all face down.

"Darlene, look at this spread of cards and point to the one that seems to be calling to you."

Darlene glared at me and then reluctantly looked down at the cards.

"They all look the same. He got to look at the faces. Everyone I'm looking at is the same."

"It's a test of fate," I said quickly. "An experiment, if you will. Just randomly point to any card."

Darlene sighed and then did as instructed. I pulled that card out and placed it on the top of the deck.

"Just like Jimmy, I'd like you to sign your name. But yours will go on the back of this random card."

"I'm not a big fan of my handwriting."

"I know the feeling," I agreed. "If you prefer, why don't you just put your initials on the back of the card?"

I held the deck in one hand and handed her the Sharpie. With a long and weary sigh, Darlene diligently wrote a large "D" across the back of the card.

"Fantastic," I said, offering way too much enthusiasm for the little work she had done. "Now let's see what fate has in store for you two. We take Darlene's card and, like Jimmy's, we let it get lost in the shuffle ..."

I quickly shuffled the deck a couple times. It may have looked like I was trying to make the trick as fair as possible, by really losing her card somewhere in the deck. In reality, I was desperately trying to remember the next step in the routine. I had already deviated a little from the original, but not so much that it would seriously impact the outcome.

I hoped.

No, the only thing that could screw it up from this point forward would be me.

I cut the cards, shuffled again, and cut them once more.

"Okay, both cards are seriously lost in the shuffle," I said. "Let's see what fate has in store for you. Will fate help us find the card Jimmy specifically chose ... or the card Darlene picked at random? Can you tell me a number that means something to both of you? A number between one and fifty-two?"

Darlene stared back at me blankly. If I had been speaking a completely foreign language—or gibberish, for that matter—I think I would have received a similar look.

"We don't have any special numbers," she began flatly, but Jimmy cut her off.

"Sure we do," he said. He let his eyes drift toward the ceiling as he thought. And then he started talking. "I won't say Darlene's age, but her birthday is September 23rd. September is the ninth month, so maybe nine? Or twenty-three?" he suggested.

He looked at Darlene but got no response. So, he continued.

"We met in junior high on October tenth, so maybe ten? We've been dating twelve years, three months and seven days, so maybe twelve, three or seven? Darlene graduated with a 3.7 GPA, so maybe three or seven? Or thirty-seven?"

Darlene was looking at him like—as the saying goes—a dog watching a ceiling fan.

But Jimmy didn't notice; he was on a roll.

"She has 20/20 vision, so twenty would be an option. The numbers on her license plate add up to twenty-seven. I'm forty days older than her. So maybe forty? When we first kissed, the time was 3:15, so maybe three? Or fifteen?

I looked over at Darlene. I don't know if her expression was shocked or surprised (I can never keep the two straight). But I suspect it was similar to the look on my face.

"Oh, my goodness, baby, you really do care," Darlene finally said, the words coming out in an emotional rasp.

"I always have," Jimmy replied. There was a little hitch in his voice as well.

"That's a lot of numbers," I said, but I wasn't really sure if the trick even needed to continue. It looked like the couple was having a bit of a breakthrough. "Do you want to pick one?"

"I'd like to pick the time we first kissed, three-fifteen," Jimmy said definitively. "But three hundred fifteen is too high."

I didn't want to be accused of leading the witness, but it looked like fate was going to smile on me. For the first time today. I just had to give it a little nudge.

"Well, maybe pick one of those two," I suggested, trying to sound casual. I had a fifty-fifty chance that Jimmy was going to make things easy for me.

"You're right," Jimmy agreed. He turned to Darlene. "Are you okay with fifteen?"

She was still staring at him, a little wide-eyed. "Sure, babe," she said in a near whisper.

"Fifteen it is," Jimmy said as he turned back to me. Their short exchange had given me exactly the cover I needed.

"Then let's count to fifteen." I looked at Jimmy, who was still holding the gun, so I turned instead to Darlene. "Do you mind putting your hand out?"

She did as instructed, but she still looked a bit shellshocked from Jimmy's long and detailed recitation of numbers connected to their relationship.

I started to deal cards face down into her hand, counting as I did. "One, two, three," I said.

They both stared down at Darlene's hand, seeming to hold their collective breath, until I got to card number thirteen. Then they looked at me. I directed their gaze down to the cards in the deck I held.

"The card on top is number fourteen," I said. "Let's see what fate has given us for the fifteenth card in the deck."

I picked up the fourteenth card, revealing the one beneath it.

The fifteenth card had a large, handwritten "D" scrawled across its back.

Without saying a word, I picked up that card and slowly turned it over.

It was the Queen of Hearts, with the name "Jimmy" carefully written across the face.

Darlene screamed. Jimmy hooted.

They hugged each other.

I sighed. The trick, despite my on-the-fly alterations, had worked.

And then—from out of nowhere—it felt like the three of us were hit by a truck and we were suddenly slammed to the floor.

6

As it turned out, we hadn't been hit by a truck.

We'd been hit by a truck *driver*.

I realized two things simultaneously as I crashed into the tile:

First, it was Chad, the truck driver, who had charged at us, knocking the three of us to the floor before landing on top of us.

And, second, I probably should have been prepared for this sudden attack, based on the short conversation we'd had about the card trick, *The Four Burglars*. As Chad had pointed out (with a wink), that trick makes a strong impact: in its dramatic conclusion, the four jacks appear from deep within the deck to make a daring escape.

In this scenario, Chad was those four Jacks, arriving at the climax of the trick in a surprising twist. And with surprising force.

At least, I think that was what he'd been thinking. There wasn't a lot of time at that moment for serious mulling or further discussion.

The four of us hit the floor hard, letting out a guttural group grunt at the point of impact.

I turned my head to see the questionably clean floor littered with playing cards ... and a gun. Jimmy must have dropped his weapon in the collision.

With the large truck driver laying atop the three of us, my movements were seriously limited. I couldn't reach the gun with my hand. But with some nominal wiggling, I realized I could make contact with it via my foot.

I gave the gun a hard kick. It spun its way across the cafe, landing near the waitress, Ruby, who was just beginning to get up off the floor.

She grabbed the gun as it soared past her, holding it up by two fingers once she'd snagged the weapon. Ruby then made a choice which would have eluded me, but which was hard to argue with: She plopped the small pistol into the water pitcher on a nearby table. The gun quickly sank into the water, drifting past the ice cubes, until it came to a rest at the bottom.

Although Chad had slammed into us with great speed and energy, getting back on our feet after that collision was another story all together.

It quickly became clear that none of us were going anywhere until he got up first. He covered us like a 250-pound tarp. However, once it was clear that the most immediate danger—the pistol—was no longer part of the picture, Chad began the slow process of getting back on his feet.

He was a big man and he had trouble finding purchase for his hands in order to push himself up off the ground. Ultimately, with one beefy paw buried deep into my back, he was finally able to struggle to his knees. I followed, besting his achievement by getting all the way to my feet before he had even progressed beyond his kneeling position.

I offered a hand to help him up, but at that point he was

already well on his way, finally reaching his six-foot-plus stature.

"Thanks for adding a nice twist to the end of that trick," I said, still trying to catch my breath. The fall hadn't knocked all the wind out of me, but it had come close.

"I got so caught up in your routine that I almost forgot the plan," he said, brushing some floor filth off the front of his shirt.

"'Plan' might be a strong word," I said. "But I admire your timing."

The other hostages were also starting to get up, the room beginning to resonate with their hubbub. More than one immediately dived for their phones.

"What do we do with him?" Chad said.

I looked down at the floor. Jimmy and Darlene were still lying side-by-side in a heap. Instead of attempting to stand, they had crawled closer together and entwined their hands. Their faces were inches apart and—although I couldn't hear anything amid the buzzing of voices which filled the room—I suspected they were cooing at each other like love birds.

"I think they're probably fine where they are," I said. "I imagine the Sheriff will be here in a manner of moments. He can deal with Jimmy."

As if in response to that prediction, I suddenly heard the sound of sirens approaching in the distance.

We looked back at the happy couple.

"You know, if you're interested in a friendly wager, I'll bet she says 'yes' the next time he proposes," Chad said.

"I think you're right."

He turned to me with a grin. "Hey, they might even invite us to the wedding."

"I'll keep an eye out for the invitation, sometime in the next two to five years. Maybe less with good behavior."

I scanned the floor, deciding to leave my scattered deck of

cards untouched; it was now part of the crime scene. I glanced at my watch. I'd probably have to give a statement of some kind to the authorities. So, I doubted I would make it to Magic Camp by supper time. With any luck, I'd roll in just before lights out.

"Looks like we might be here for a bit," I said to Chad. Through the front window I could see two squad cars as they pulled into the café's parking lot. "I don't have any more cards, but if we've got four quarters between us, I can show you David Roth's version of The Sympathetic Coins. It's a pretty sweet routine."

"And don't tell me: You learned it directly from David Roth?"

I shrugged. "If it's any consolation, it wasn't one-on-one. They were maybe four of us in the room at the time."

"Eli, I know we've just met, but I've got to be honest: I think I could grow to hate you."

With that, we headed back to our booth.

I don't know how much time passed—we quickly went deep into a discussion of the subtleties of the trick—but we stopped long enough to watch through the front window as Jimmy was loaded into one of the squad cars. Darlene was with him up to the last second, and then stood there throwing kisses at the car as it pulled out of the lot and headed toward the highway.

Chad and I resumed our discussion about the coin trick, waiting for our turns to be interviewed by the Sheriff's deputies.

With refreshened coffee courtesy of Ruby, and a couple terrific cheeseburgers thrown in, it turned out to be a surprisingly pleasant way to spend an afternoon.

THE SQUARE CIRCLE

"He was a man of square deceit, and his crooked schemes never failed to come full circle"
   —Edgar Allan Poe, The Tell-Tale Heart

1

His timing could not have been worse.

For the first instance in, I don't know, *forever*, the store was packed.

It must have been one of those perfect storm situations. We host a monthly magic meeting in our back room. Attendance is usually, at best, spotty. However, on this particular Monday night, the turnout had been substantial. I'm not sure if Mercury was in retrograde (a popular explanation provided by my wife, Megan) or if every magician in the club decided this was the <u>one</u> meeting they couldn't miss. Whatever the reason, we'd had an unusually large crowd pile into our cramped back room. Many of the attendees had then opted to stick around after the meeting, to check out new products and spend whatever cash might be burning a hole in their pocket for the latest tricks and gaffes.

Consequently, when Homicide Detective Fred Hutton entered Chicago Magic, he was simply one of the throng and there was no one to greet him. I was in the midst of demonstrating a classic trick from Tenyo. And my uncle Harry was arguing with a customer who wanted to return what he claimed was a faulty packet of flash paper.

"It doesn't work?" Harry repeated, making no attempt to remove any level of annoyance from his voice. "What do you mean it doesn't work? It's flash paper. That's like saying an apple doesn't work."

I was trying to monitor the level of frustration at Harry's end of the counter, while I went through the steps of demonstrating a fun device designed to make a tiny Statue of Liberty disappear. It was half magic trick, half toy. I glanced over at Homicide Detective Fred Hutton, who gave me the slightest of nods. It was a look which said, *"I get it, you're busy, I'll wait."*

At least I think that's what his expression said. It could have just as easily been saying, *"I am really annoyed at being ignored and I promise, you will pay for this."*

He was a tough man to read, even at the best of times.

I handed off the Statue of Liberty trick to the potential customer, so they could try it out on their own. Then I made a quick scan of the room, to see if there were any other fires which needed putting out. Harry's flash paper situation seemed to have calmed a bit, once the customer admitted he had lied about having worked with the product in the past. With that admission out in the open, Harry had instantly switched into mentor mode. He was now instructing the customer on the proper method for drying flash paper—which is always wet when purchased—before using it.

My friend Nathan—who, thank goodness, had made a rare appearance at this evening's meeting—had stuck around and was pitching in as well. He seemed to have his end of the room under control. He was offering suggestions to two teens, helping them decide which magic book they were going to purchase together. They were excited because their pooled resources gave them greater-than-usual buying power. He was steering them toward Tommy Wonder's two-volume set, *The*

Books of Wonder, which was exactly what I would have done in that situation. A complete win-win for the two kids: they would each walk out of the store with a classic volume in their hands, along with the prospect of easy access to the other book.

And it was nice to see some possible revenue coming from that bookcase, as it had felt like quite a while since I'd sold any books.

I crossed the room to Homicide Detective Fred Hutton, who had found a bit of open space near the shelf of gag gifts. As I approached, he was examining a pair of chattering teeth. When he saw me headed his way, he set the toothy device back on the shelf. However, moving it must have jostled its inner workings. And so, the teeth began to chatter happily on the shelf, vibrating dangerously toward the edge. I was able to reach out and grab the toy in midair, just before it vibrated itself right onto the hard tile floor below.

"I must have switched it on, somehow," he said. There was a rare note of apology in his otherwise flat monotone.

"Not to worry. Those chattering teeth appear to have a mind of their own. A lot of things seem to set them off: someone slams the door or when I close the cash register drawer too hard. And, on more than one occasion when I've been alone here in the store, they've just suddenly started wildly chattering out of nowhere. I mean, it might have been months since anyone touched them, and then out of the blue they're vibrating and making a racket. Pretty spooky."

"If no one has touched them in months, why do you bother stocking them?"

That question was Homicide Detective Fred Hutton in a nutshell: Give him some fascinating fact about the world around us and he could instantly reduce it to one of his patented baffling *Is he insulting me?* statements.

"You could well ask that of ninety percent of the items in

this store. It's a daily struggle not to think about it," I said. "Can I help you with something?"

"Yes, I'm hoping you can," he said, switching seamlessly into business mode. Which, to be fair, was pretty indistinguishable from all of his other modes. He flipped open a small black notebook and quickly paged through the first couple of sheets. "I'm investigating a missing persons case," he said slowly, which offered me a space for a quick interruption.

"Missing persons? I thought you were... *exclusive*... to Homicide," I said. I had struggled to find the right word and felt I had at least come close.

"Things are quiet at present. I'm lending a hand. Plus, you'd be surprised at how many missing persons cases often morph into a matter for homicide. And when your name popped up on the witness list, it made sense for me to be the one to stop by and chat. Given our relationship and all."

His use of the word *relationship* almost made me miss the other key word in his statement: *witness*. I was torn as to which word to explore further. Each one appeared to contain hidden depths.

Did we have an actual *relationship*? He was married to my ex-wife; his involvement with her was the reason Deirdre and I had gotten divorced. Did that mean that Homicide Detective Fred Hutton and I also were in a relationship? And, if so, how would you define it?

After a momentary hesitation, I decided this was not the rabbit hole worth diving into on this particular evening. I opted instead to focus my attention on that second significant word from his statement.

"Witness?" I repeated. "I'm a witness in a missing persons case?"

"Witness might be a strong term," he agreed. "Let's just say we're hoping you can corroborate an alibi. And help us solidify a timeline for the missing woman."

"Sure thing."

"Her name is Heather Clark," he said as he reviewed his notes. "Her last known point of contact was a phone call she made to her husband. He said he was here, in your store, when he received the call."

"Heather Clark," I repeated. "It doesn't ring any bells."

"Her husband is Matt Clark."

I shook my head.

"He said he was here two days ago—Saturday—with his nephews. They were here for a magic lesson?"

Suddenly I realized who he was talking about.

"Ah, yes, the Claxton twins. Their uncle has brought them in for their last few lessons. Their mom is a single parent and I guess her brother was helping her out. Now that you mention it, I remember he introduced himself as Matt. I don't think I ever heard his last name."

"So, Mr. Clark and his nephews were in fact here two days ago—Saturday—between 2:00 p.m. and 4:00 p.m.?"

"They were indeed," I said. "I think we even went late on that one. It was a big lesson. We started working on the Square Circle."

"I'm sorry?"

"It's a trick, an illusion," I explained. "The Claxton twins are working on their magic act. It's pretty cute, actually. I'm not sure it will be as adorable when they're thirty, but at age ten it's charming."

"And you're teaching them their tricks?"

I nodded. "In some cases, when they want to add something new—we look at possible options. Like in this case, the Square Circle. Otherwise, we just work on refining their current repertoire, honing and sanding."

"So, you've added 'teacher' to your CV?"

I laughed. "I don't think I have an actual Cee or a Vee. Only

once in my life have I put together a résumé. And we both
know how that turned out."

He nodded. There had been a time, not too long before,
when I had actually applied for—and been hired—for a job as
part of a case he was working on. Homicide Detective Fred
Hutton had saved my life on that one—literally—but, oddly
enough, it rarely came up in conversation. Another odd twist in
our continually evolving *relationship*.

"Yes," I continued. "I'm moving away from strictly
performing and starting to do some teaching and consulting."

"And last Saturday afternoon was spent working on the
Squared Circle with Matt Clark's nephews?"

"The Square Circle," I corrected. "They call it that because
it involves a square box and a round tube thing ..."

I realized showing him the device would be simpler than
trying to describe it. The illusion was easy to find, as it was right
where I'd left it at the far end of the counter. I guess that's the
benefit of never putting anything away.

"It's a pretty slick illusion," I continued as I adjusted the
box's position. I had moved behind the counter and Homicide
Detective Fred Hutton had stepped to the other side of the
display. We had, somehow, effortlessly slid into customer and
demonstrator mode. "And it could be perfect for the twins' act.
It's got two pieces: the 'square' is this square box, closed on
three sides but with this see-through grate on the front. The
other piece—the 'circle'—is this colorful tube, which you can
slide into the box easily through the top."

As I said this, I held up the tube, to show it was in fact
empty. I then slid it into the box. Although the interior of the
case was black, the bright tube was now clearly visible through
the lattice work in the front of the box.

"The trick basically consists of magically pulling different
items out of the apparently empty tube," I said.

I demonstrated by reaching into the tube and pulling out a

long string of colorful silks. I then pulled the tube out of the box and held it up, to again prove it was empty. Then I put it back into the box and once again pulled another item from the seemingly empty tube; in this case, it was a small bouquet of plastic flowers. I handed them to the detective.

"Oh, I see. So, the name The Square Circle really has nothing to do with the classic math problem of squaring the circle?" he said as he casually examined the plastic flowers. "You know, sacred geometry, transcendental numbers, pi, the golden ratio and all that?"

I shrugged. "It's all Greek to me."

"Indeed, it <u>was</u> all Greek. And if it weren't for modern algebra, it would still be a mystery." He uttered a rare chuckle. "But I'm not telling you anything you don't already know."

The fact was, I had no idea how much I didn't know on that topic, among an embarrassment of others. I sensed it was a lot. But I nodded in agreement as I placed the colorful tube back into the box.

"So, where was Matt Clark while you were working with his nephews?"

I gestured across the room, to the large bookcase which took up much of one of the shop's four walls. "He mostly hung out by the books. He'd pull up a chair and read while he waited."

"He brought a book with him?"

"No, he'd take one off the shelf and look through it."

"And you're okay with people reading books that they're not buying?"

"It's a long-standing store tradition," I said with a laugh. "Harry has always had a policy of letting people really examine a book or take it home, sort of on loan, to see if they want to eventually buy it. That's the reason for the chair over there. In fact, that's why I put that placard above the bookcase, lo those many years ago."

I gestured to the sign which I'd made and hung over the bookcase back when I was a teen. It read *"793.8"*

"That's the library classification for magic books," I explained. "I figured if Harry was going to treat this place like a lending library, then we might as well have the area properly classified."

Homicide Detective Fred Hutton nodded. "I see. Just like *364.1* is the library classification for crimes and offenses," he said dryly. He glanced back down at his notes. "So, he just sat over there, looking through books?"

I nodded. "Actually, just one book, I think."

"Every time?"

I thought about it. "I believe so."

"And on this most recent Saturday, did he receive any phone calls?"

I thought back. It was only two days ago, but I'd taught three other lessons since then and everything sort of blurred together. "Yes, he did," I finally said. "I remember, because he was on the phone for a couple minutes or so. And then he came over and asked the twins if they wanted to say 'hi' to their aunt."

"And did they? Say 'hi' to their aunt?"

I shook my head. "They were very focused on the correct handling of the tube at that point," I explained. "It can be a little tricky."

"Well, it is a trick after all."

Was he making a joke? With him, it was impossible to tell.

"And how did Matt Clark respond to that? The twins' lack of interest in talking to their aunt?"

"He just chuckled and returned to his call. And the next time I looked over, he was once again in the chair, reading."

"I see." He continued to look through his notes.

"Does that fit the timeline?"

He nodded slowly. "Yes, in theory. According to her phone records, Heather Clark placed a phone call from the Mall of America at approximately 2:45 p.m. Data from the towers places her at or around that location for about another hour. And then the phone traveled West on Highway 494 for a few miles. At that point, either the battery died, or the phone was shut off."

"And you haven't found her car?"

"That's the odd thing. Her car was discovered in the Mall of America parking lot yesterday. Probably where she parked it on Saturday. It even still had the keys in it."

"But no trace of her?"

"Nothing yet."

"That's weird."

"It is indeed." He took another look through his notes and then shut his notebook. "Okay, thanks. I think that's all we need for now."

I was tempted to employ Harry's response when people used the royal "we" ("What, have you got a mouse in your pocket?"), but felt now wasn't the appropriate time to do that with Homicide Detective Fred Hutton. I'm not sure there ever would be such a time.

He was halfway across the store when he turned back.

"Do you have any idea which book?" He gestured toward the bookcase, where Nathan was just wrapping up his sale with the two teens. "Which book Matt Clark was reading?"

I looked from him to the bookcase and back to him. Did I know? I think it might have had a white or a very light cover, but I wasn't certain. Nothing jumped immediately to mind, so I gave him my most truthful response: I shrugged.

"Thanks again," he said and was out the door.

I walked over to the large bookcase, passing Nathan and his two customers as they headed toward the cash register. Each one was carrying one of the two Tommy Wonder volumes. I smiled. They were about to get a personal tour of Oz with one of the greatest wizards of all time.

I stood in front of the bookcase, repeating the detective's question in my head. Which book had Matt Clark been reading?

I had no idea.

2

"You had a late night."

I squinted up at Megan, who was looking down at me, a cup of coffee poised in her hand.

"We had a bigger than usual magic meeting turnout, followed by intense shopping from rabid customers. Still not sure why."

"Well, Mercury is in retrograde," Megan offered.

I sat up and took the steaming cup from her. The milky white liquid within told me it had been poured to my exacting specifications: Lots of chocolate creamer and just enough coffee to give the hot beverage an oh-so slight coffee flavor.

"Thanks," I said after my first long sip. "There might be something to that whole Mercury in Gatorade thing, though. I had a visit from Homicide Detective Fred Hutton, of all people."

"A social visit?"

I nearly did a classic spit-take. "That seems highly unlikely."

"I don't know. I think he likes you more than he lets on."

"Well, the most I get from him is intense indifference. And that's on a good day."

"So, why did he stop by?"

"Something about a missing persons case. Apparently, the woman who is missing, her husband is the uncle of the Claxton twins. You know, the pair I've been giving lessons to."

"Are those the two who got into a tussle on stage during their act?"

I smiled at the memory. It had been about three years ago when the Claxton twins made their first stage appearance during the Gala Show at our local magic convention. Although their act had started out well, at some point there had been a disagreement about who was supposed to be wielding the magic wand. A fistfight ensued—granted, because they were seven, it had been more of a slap-fest—and adults had to step in and pull them apart.

They had matured a bit since then, but I didn't see them working as a double act for the rest of their lives. Uncle Harry had his own opinion, which was a tad more optimistic.

"Some of the most successful show business teams hated each other off stage. It adds a lovely tension to an act. Don't sound the death knell on that young team just yet. The jury is still out on those two."

I had my doubts but kept them to myself.

"So, their mother is a missing person?" Megan asked, pulling me back to the here and now.

I shook my head as I took another sip.

"No, it's their aunt. Their mother's brother. His wife. He's brought the twins in for their lessons a handful of times over the last few months."

"And his wife is missing?"

"Since Saturday. She called him from the Mall of America —he was in the store when he took the call—and then she disappeared."

"The husband did it."

"I suppose that's the common explanation," I agreed. "But he's got a good alibi—me—and the phone records also exonerate him."

"Doesn't matter. I've seen more than my share of Netflix true crime documentaries. The husband always did it."

"You know what Uncle Harry says: all generalizations are wrong, including the generalization that all generalizations are wrong ..."

"Speaking of Uncle Harry, he still doesn't have a clue, right?"

I recognized the sudden conversational shift. These were not uncommon with Megan. In fact, if anything, they were the norm. I had once considered getting her a t-shirt which read, *Sharp Turns Ahead.* But wiser heads prevailed.

"He remains clueless," I reported. "He is currently figuratively in the dark as to his impending surprise party."

"We need to keep it that way."

"We'll see," I said. I wasn't convinced it was possible. It was like trying to keep a secret from Sherlock Holmes. "The more people who know, the more likely it is someone will let something slip."

"The husband did it. My money's on him."

It took a second for me to realize we were back to our previous topic.

"Are we betting on this?"

"No, that would be sick. But if we were—which we're not—I would win."

Before I could offer a rebuttal, she was out of the room and onto her next morning chore. I sipped the remains of my coffee and considered her adamant statement.

Had the husband done it? And, if so, what had he done?

* * *

"Wow, we're getting our fill of the Sutton-Hutton clan around here this week," I said as I looked up from straightening some liquor bottles behind the bar. My ex-wife (who had hyphenated her name when remarrying, giving her the always amusing name Deirdre Sutton-Hutton), had quietly appeared and was leaning on the bar. She was dressed, as always, in a smart and well-tailored coat and skirt combination, befitting her role as one of the city's key Assistant District Attorneys.

"I first went into the magic store, but Nathan said to check over here. You still haven't found someone to tend bar in the afternoon?"

I gestured to the near-empty saloon, which Megan and I had purchased the previous year. The only customers were Uncle Harry and a couple of his pals, seated at their normal spot in a back corner. "I can't make the finances work to hire any help," I admitted.

"Isn't that what you used to say about the magic store?"

"And that was true until Nathan took over. Turns out, he's quite the salesman. Nathan could sell ..." I struggled to remember the full aphorism. "Ice or coal or refrigerators or something to Eskimos or to people in Newcastle who already own or manufacture whatever it is he's selling..." I abandoned the concept in mid-thought. "You get the idea. So, what can I do for you?"

She glanced around, dropping her volume as she did. "I'm actually here for Harry." She pulled a pale pink envelope from her purse. "I'm stopping by to give him his birthday card."

"No, no," I sputtered, trying to keep my voice down while dramatically opposing her idea. "We can't mention his birthday. He'll figure it out."

She shook her head. "On the contrary, if no one mentions his birthday, he will <u>know</u> something is up. You have to think like he thinks."

"I am intimately familiar with how he thinks," I hissed

through clenched teeth. "Historically, any time I thought I was two steps ahead of Harry, I invariably discovered he was actually miles ahead of me. And seated comfortably, drinking a glass of ginger ale, when I finally caught up to him."

"Trust me, I've got this," she said as she turned to head toward Harry's table in the back.

From my position behind the bar, I couldn't stop her even if I'd wanted to. My days of leaping over a bar in a single bound were long behind me, if they'd ever existed in the first place. Of course, even if the bar hadn't been between us, I knew it was fruitless to stand between Deirdre and something she's decided to do. It was her way or the highway. This was true when she'd said she wanted to get married. And equally true when she decided it was time to get divorced.

She was halted in her progress by a sudden beeping emanating from her purse. She stopped, clearly annoyed by the interruption. She pulled her phone out and glared at it.

"Oh, Barry, give it a rest," she hissed. She turned back to me. "They've hired a new guy in the office, an assistant for all the ADAs..."

"You mean an Assistant to the Assistant District Attorneys?" I suggested. "That's a mouthful. Does Barry's title continue around the back on his business card?"

"If he keeps this up, Barry's not going to be around long enough to even get a business card." She looked at her phone's screen again. "Another unnecessary message, to let me know that he's done the simple thing I asked him to do. And odds are, he did it wrong. But that doesn't stop Barry from texting me constantly throughout the day with pointless updates." She sighed as she deposited her phone back into her purse. "Another one of those idiot go-getters in the alleged justice system who consistently confuses the idea of <u>fast</u> with the concept of <u>efficient</u>."

"I'm afraid that sort isn't unique to your line of work, my

dear." This came from Uncle Harry, who was heading toward the bar, his empty glass in hand. "The world is full of people like that, racing from goal to goal without recognizing the value of doing it correctly, as opposed to doing it quickly. The magic community has, I believe, more than its fair share of that type."

He set the glass on the bar between us. "Barkeep, can I trouble you for a refill on my ginger ale?"

"I was just headed back to check on you guys," I lied. I grabbed the glass and smoothly slid open the door to the ice drawer.

"And let's keep that ice-to-beverage ratio a bit more in favor of the ginger ale this time, be a good fellow."

"You'd think someone who gets his drinks for free might be a little less demanding."

"Yes, you might think that," Harry said, and then he turned to Deirdre. "And what brings you by this fine establishment today?"

She held out the envelope. "A birthday greeting," she said. "I wasn't sure I'd be able to get over here on the actual day. And I didn't trust the post office to get it to you on time."

"A birthday card, how lovely, thank you so much." He held up the envelope so that I could see it. "It's nice to see that someone around here remembers my birthday."

"Your birthday is several days away and it's unlikely you'll let any of us forget it. I'm surprised you haven't hung up a banner in here."

He wasn't even listening to me as he slid the card from the envelope. He chuckled at the front of the card, flipped it open and read the inscription, and then looked at the cover again.

"Oh, that's delightful," he said, still grinning. "What a relief it is to get a card at my age that doesn't end with a not-so-veiled joke about my impending death or supposed lack of sexual prowess. Thank you, Deirdre. Thank you for remembering my birthday. It's a landmark one, you know."

"I know, Harry," Deirdre said with a smile. "It's a big one."

Over the years I'd come to realize most of the smiles I'd seen on Deirdre had been when Harry was around. Clearly, she had no trouble admitting her affection for the old guy. It was just with husbands and ex-husbands where showing warmth appeared to be a struggle.

"I've got to show the fellows," Harry said as he reached for the now-full glass (twenty percent ice, eighty percent ginger ale) I'd set on the counter. "Thanks so much, Deirdre."

He shuffled his way back to his cronies and moments later we could hear them chuckling over the birthday card. Deirdre turned to me, not even bothering to tamper her smugness.

"You see, he hasn't got a clue."

"I'm not so sure," I said. "Planning a surprise party for Harry is like ..." I paused, trying hard to complete the metaphor. Or the simile. Or whatever it was I was struggling with. "Well, it's like planning a surprise party for Harry," I finally sputtered. "It's the ultimate magic trick. He's wily. He's sees everything."

"Perhaps, but this time I think we may have him."

"I'd bet you on that, but I think I've got a wager going with Megan about this missing persons thing your husband asked me about. Any new information?"

She shook her head. "No new leads," she said. "However, we did learn there's a million-dollar life insurance policy, purchased within the last year."

"Well, that's a bit of a smoking gun, isn't it?"

"Yes, that's what we thought at first. But we were wrong. Turns out, the million-dollar policy was for when <u>he</u> dies. The policy the couple had on the missing wife was only for $500,000."

"Okay, so it wasn't about insurance. How's his story holding up?"

"Well, according to you, he was in the magic shop from 2:00 p.m. to well after 4:00 p.m."

"Yes. And he received a call from his wife while he was there," I added.

"A neighbor saw their car pulling out of the garage at about the time Heather Clark was said to be headed toward the Mall of America, which was about noon. And another neighbor saw Matt out for a jog and they think it was Saturday morning. Or maybe Saturday afternoon. Or maybe Sunday. Or it might have been Friday. I hate eyewitnesses."

"Megan insists the husband did it."

Deirdre smiled. "Well, statistically, she is not wrong. Although I'm not sure that's the way this one went down."

"What do you mean? You have your own theory?"

She settled onto one of the bar stools and I moved down the counter to listen.

"Here's what we know: She left her car at the Mall of America. With the keys in it, suggesting she was either addlebrained or wanted someone to steal the car. Unfortunately, the honest patrons of the Mall of America let her down on that one," Deirdre began.

"The more I think about it, the more I believe she took advantage of the light rail that stops at the Mall. She put on a wig and jumped on a train. Just one stop away is the airport. Then, using an assumed name and passport, she headed off to destinations unknown. I think if we do some investigation—a bit of financial forensics—we may find some form of embezzlement at the investment firm where she worked. Of course, that's just my theory."

I thought about this for a long moment. "What about her phone?" I finally said. "How did it head down Highway 494 West if she was heading in the other direction to the airport?"

"I'm not sure on that point," Deirdre admitted. "Not sure we will ever know. But in my mind, for the time being at least, this is a wife who took it on the lam. Pure and simple."

Before I could respond, she turned and gave me a sharp look. Probably because she knew I could never leave that Oscar Wilde phrase alone. Over the years, I don't know how many variations I had done on it in front of her.

I decided to let this be one of those times when I left it alone.

3

I was staring intently at the Square Circle illusion when Harry walked into the shop. He stood in the doorway and looked at me for a long moment.

"Eli, you realize I'm sure, that the Square Circle is not <u>literally</u> a self-working trick," he said with a wry chuckle. "Even in the best of hands."

"I know, I know," I mumbled. I stood up and stretched, not sure how long I had been sitting, staring at the ornate box and the brightly colored tube. The manner in which my muscles cried out at the sudden movement suggested it had been a while. "The Claxton twins are on the fence about buying this thing, and I don't blame them. I've been trying to come up with some ideas for a way for two people to do it. Without making one of them merely the assistant."

"A sore point with the twins, is it? The role of assistant?"

"The sorest of points," I said. "They each have to be the star at every moment in the show, or they won't put a trick in the act."

Harry chuckled. "I may need to adjust my previous assessment. That doesn't bode well for a long-term career."

"You're telling me. Of course, I have no desire to sell them something they're not going to use. But it bugs me that I can't come up with some ideas. Or one idea. Even a crummy idea would be a welcome sight at this point."

"Well, if you're looking for something unique and coming up short, don't beat yourself up too badly. To create a new presentation for the Square Circle would be quite the challenge for anyone. The trick has been around for a long, long time, you know. A lot of creative minds have been down this same path and hit a similar dead end."

"I suppose you're right," I agreed. "Maybe the trick is just too simple to make it work with two people."

I began to gather up the pieces of the illusion, planning to set the whole thing back on the shelf, to await another possible sales opportunity. Or, more likely, to gather dust like everything else in the store. And then suddenly, Harry grabbed my arm.

"Wait, wait," he said quickly. "That might be the key: It's too simple to work with two people. Be a good fellow and grab that portable table, will you? The one with the fringe skirt. We still have it, right?"

"We do indeed."

I knew exactly where it was, because I had to move it every time I needed to pull an item off one of the shelves in the back room. Why I just didn't fold it up or find a permanent storage space for the skinny table is in itself a view in miniature of how I managed all the inventory in the store: there simply wasn't a logical system.

I disappeared behind the curtain and re-appeared moments later, carrying the small table in front of me. Harry indicated that he wanted it positioned by the counter where the Square Circle pieces now sat.

"Okay, I'm making this up as I go along, so bear with me," he said. He repositioned the table so that it was evenly spaced between the two of us. "Let's say our two magicians enter from either side of the stage. You've got the tube, I've got the box. The table is standing here, pre-set. I hold up the box, revealing that it is—in fact—completely empty."

He did just that, and then set the box on the small table between us.

"Now, you take the tube and set it in the box."

I did as instructed. The colorful tube was now visible through the grate in the front of the box.

"At that moment, my character takes umbrage, because you have not demonstrated your tube is empty," Harry continued. "I gesture for you to do that, and you do. You pull the tube from the box and show the audience that it is in fact empty."

I followed his instructions and completed those simple steps.

"You then return the tube to its place in the box, wait a beat, and then pull an object out of the seemingly empty tube."

I pulled a long stream of colorful silks from within the tube.

"My character is surprised and a little outraged at this," Harry said. "And I insist that you show me the tube is empty."

I did just that, demonstrating to both Harry and the non-existent audience that the tube was empty. And then once again I set the tube inside the box.

"This creates more annoyance from my character at that afront," Harry continued. "I peer into the box. I look under the stand. I even go so far as to pull the shimmering skirt from around the base of the table."

He yanked the skirt off in one fluid motion, which was accompanied by a loud ripping sound. Harry looked a little surprised.

"Sorry about that," he said sheepishly. "Hasn't that skirt always been held in place with Velcro?

"I know the table you're thinking of," I said. "It's not this one. However, from a comedic point of view, the ripping sound effect is a nice touch. I suggest we leave it in."

"Agreed."

"I suppose at that point, I pull another object from the tube?"

Harry nodded and I did just that, producing the same plastic bouquet Homicide Detective Fred Hutton had held when he first examined the illusion.

"Exactly. You continue to cluelessly produce items, and I continue to fume. Not unlike the multiplying bottle routine that Morgan & West do so brilliantly. At a certain point, the magic takes a backseat to the comedic interplay between the two characters."

Ah, yes, I thought. Yet another example of Harry's ongoing love affair with Morgan & West.

After seeing the pair perform at a magic convention several months back, the British duo Morgan & West had become Harry's go-to example of how to perform magic: How to set up a routine. How to interact with the audience. How to create impossible-seeming magic while offering exceptional comic repartee. Harry mentioned them so often, and with such high praise, I couldn't help but be a bit jealous of his affection for them. I felt like an only child who was suddenly upstaged by two highly gifted British siblings.

We played with the trick for several more minutes, adding beats and small props, creating the rough outline of a strong routine.

"The nice thing about this approach is that it's perfectly balanced, with both of them getting the same amount of stage time," I said when we stopped for a break.

"Indeed," Harry agreed. "Of course, you need to come up with some more story beats and a boffo ending. Plus, you'll need to find a killer piece of music…"

I nodded. "I have a couple thoughts already." I mentally began to flip through my favorite music play lists. "This is fantastic. Thanks."

"Always happy to assist in the creation of new magical presentations," Harry said. "It keeps me young."

Harry's reference to his age reminded me I had a super-secret errand to run. I headed over to the cash register, looking for something which was supposed to be there. It wasn't immediately visible.

"You lose something?" Harry asked.

It was impossible to slip anything past him. He was heading toward the door I'd installed a few weeks back, which offered easy access between the magic shop and the bar next door. I struggled to come up with a quick and plausible response and —with no options immediately accessible—I settled for the path of least resistance. The truth.

"Nathan said I could borrow his car. He was going to leave the keys by the register." I scanned the area again, still not seeing the small key ring.

"Perhaps he meant in the register," Harry suggested. "Why do you need Nathan's car?"

I ignored the question and punched the old, sticky buttons to open the register. The drawer slid open, revealing a small stack of bills, an old box of TicTacs, a kazoo, some ancient poker chips, and an *I Like Ike* button. Nestled on top of all this detritus was Nathan's key ring.

"Here we go," I said as I grabbed the keys and slammed the drawer shut.

Across the room, the chattering teeth on the Gag & Gift shelf were triggered to life by the sound. Harry reached out— probably more out of habit than anything else—and quieted the noisy toy.

"Why do you need Nathan's car?" Harry repeated. "Why does the fellow with a tiny Mini-Cooper require the use of a Morris Minor Wagon? Hauling something large, are we? Perhaps an over-sized birthday cake?"

"Nothing that festive, I'm afraid." I stammered. "Plus, you

said you didn't want any fuss made about your birthday. Are you and Franny planning anything special?"

"I said I didn't want any <u>unnecessary</u> fuss," Harry replied, not taking the bait to shift the direction of the conversation. "So why do you need the Morris Minor wagon?"

He was persisting like a dog with a bone. The only way out was to fabricate something credible. He took this long moment of silence to make some slight adjustments to several items on the dusty Gag & Gift shelf. I racked my brain and finally came up with the closest thing to plausible I could find on such short notice.

"Shelves," I suddenly blurted. "Megan found a deal on some shelves for her store and needs me to pick them up. Obviously, they won't fit in the Mini-Cooper."

"Well, obviously," Harry agreed. "You can barely fit two people in that clown car, let alone shelving."

"True enough," I said with a laugh which didn't come out like my normal laugh. I could feel myself begin to perspire. "Hey, do you mind watching the shop for an hour or so?"

I had planned on just closing the store for my errand, but hoped this sudden change in topic might throw Harry further off the scent. I also realized there was an intrinsic value in knowing exactly where he would be for the next couple of hours.

"I watched this grubby old place for forty-plus years," Harry said as he modified his course, heading away from the door. "Can't hurt to watch it for a couple more hours."

We swapped places behind the counter, and I quickly made my way out of the shop.

I wanted to disappear before he could generate yet another series of probing questions I didn't want to answer.

4

"Does Harry have a clue?"

"Harry <u>always</u> has a clue," I muttered. "Harry always has all the clues. I'm not so sure how long we can keep this whole thing a secret."

Laurence Baxter offered a murmur of agreement.

We were standing in the baggage claim area in the Minneapolis/St. Paul airport, as luggage from the just-landed London plane began to drop heavily onto the revolving carousel. A few of the more annoying arriving passengers had made a tight circle around the carousel, so that only those in their inner group could spot their bags. Had they just stepped back four feet, we'd all have a clear view of the arriving luggage. But of course, none of them were willing to do that. The needs of the few seemed to outweigh the needs of the many, I guess. This was just one of innumerable human habits which had long ago soured me to air travel specifically and human beings in general.

Next to me was the passenger from that flight I had come to pick-up: Laurence Baxter.

I looked over at my older companion and shook my head in

mild disbelief. Here I was, standing next to one of the most famous people in Great Britain, and no one around us seemed to have a clue. Well, that wasn't entirely true; a few of the plane's other passengers threw an occasional glance our way, but I suspected the glow of his celebrity may have dimmed in the wake of their six-hour flight and their resulting jet lag. However, the continuous stream of people moving past us seemed completely oblivious to the major luminary in their midst.

For his part, Baxter seemed not to mind he was going unnoticed. He looked tanned and fit, and not just for his age. He <u>always</u> looked tanned and fit; never a hair out of place, never an askew crease in his trousers, never the least bit of sag in his collar.

Before I'd first met Laurence Baxter many years before, my uncle Harry had offered this perspective on his old friend:

"Eli, just think of Baxter as the Johnny Carson of England," Harry had explained. "Carson, in his heyday, was one of the most recognized people in the United States. In his own way, Baxter fills that role in Great Britain. A beloved television magician and presenter, he is recognized everywhere ... until he travels past Dover. At that point, he is just like me: another old man with a few tricks up his sleeve and a worn deck of cards in his pocket."

"Do you want to grab a chair while we wait for the crowd to clear?" I suggested to Baxter. "I don't think we're in a rush. I'm not sure the other plane has even landed yet."

Somehow the fates had smiled on me. With one flight coming from London and the other from Las Vegas, I was sure I'd be making two trips to the airport to shuttle our out-of-town visitors. However, fortunately, both flights were due to arrive within minutes of each other. Perhaps Mercury was in retrograde after all.

Baxter cocked his head to one side. "I think you may be

mistaken as to the arrival of that other plane, Eli," he said. "I'm clearly hearing one singular voice which could only belong to our friend, Mr. Templeton."

He turned to his left and I followed his gaze. It took several seconds for me to separate the loud voice from the continuous din of the Baggage Claim area, but then I heard it. Baxter was right: It was clearly Roy Templeton and we were somewhere within the sound of his voice, which actually didn't narrow things down all that much. His voice could encompass a wide area indeed.

A few more seconds of scanning and I finally spotted him, two carousels over. He was headed our way, weighed down by a backpack and dragging two large suitcases behind him. His wife, Roxanne, followed with a slim suitcase of her own. She spotted us and steered Roy in our direction.

The contrast between Roy Templeton and Laurence Baxter could not be more severe. Baxter was all British stateliness and calm. Templeton was a whirling dervish of a man, a performer who didn't leave his comic persona on stage, but lived it twenty-four hours a day. He was a lot of fun for short bursts, but I had found he quickly exhausted me. I'm not sure how his wife, Roxanne, put up with him. I've seen thirteen-year-old boys all hopped up on sugar and Red Bull calmer than Roy Templeton.

"Mr. Baxter, Mr. Marks Junior, delighted, delighted," Roy said, quickly shaking our hands. "You remember the old ball and chain?"

"Roxanne, good to see you," Baxter said, pushing past Roy to give Roxanne a warm hug. "How do you live with him?"

"I ask myself that same question on a daily basis," she replied with a laugh, reaching out and giving my a hand a squeeze while maintaining her hug with Baxter. "We would have been here sooner, but our excess luggage took longer than expected. Cher here needed to pack enough costume changes for a world tour. We once traveled with Siegfried & Roy, and my dear husband required twice the luggage they did. And they were traveling with two tigers."

"And you get by with just one bag?" Baxter pointed out, noting the contrast.

"Yes, but she carries far more emotional baggage than I do," Roy snapped.

"I have more emotional baggage because of you, dear," she said with a smile. She turned to Baxter and me. "As you can see, the road company of *Who's Afraid of Virginia Wolff* is unchanged from the last time you saw us."

"And we wouldn't want it any other way," Baxter said. "Eli, I believe my luggage has arrived. It's the fuchsia one, just going past now."

I spotted the bag he meant and pushed my way through the remaining crowd to grab it.

Minutes later, we were packed into Nathan's Morris Minor wagon and headed toward the hotel I'd booked for our three super-secret out-of-town guests.

* * *

"So, Eli, are you currently embroiled in any mind-bending mysteries?"

The question came from Roy Templeton who, with Roxanne, was currently in the back seat of the roomy vehicle. Well, it was roomy to me. After years of driving a Mini Cooper, sitting inside anything larger than a refrigerator box seemed spacious.

"Embroiled? Not so much. Things have been pretty quiet lately."

"I still tell people about our adventure in London all the time," Roy said. I glanced into the rearview mirror. He was grinning broadly. "How you solved those murders and all. Pretty spiffy."

"It might have been more spiffy—safety wise—to solve the mystery about five minutes sooner than I did, but thanks," I said.

It has been pointed out to me that I often tended to come up with the right answer, but nearly always a few minutes past when it really might have been helpful to do so. I was working on not doing that anymore.

"Well, Harry is very proud of you," Baxter added. "He has shared a few of your adventures in his all-too infrequent emails."

"Having known you since you were a kid, I can't help but think of you as that famous teenage sleuth," Roxanne said. "What's the name?"

"Nancy Drew?" Roy suggested.

"No, you idiot," Roxanne said, giving his arm a playful slap. "The other one. Encyclopedia Brown."

"They should update those books," Roy said. "Call him Wikipedia Brown. Every time he comes up with a solution, someone rewrites the clues! Ha!" Roy provided the laugh he felt the joke deserved.

"There is a case my ex-wife is currently working on," I said. "It has certain interesting characteristics."

I launched into an abbreviated recitation of the facts concerning Heather Clark's disappearance. When I concluded, all three of my passengers were silent. But not for long.

"The husband did it," Roxanne said definitively.

"You and my wife share that belief," I said.

"I've got to go along with Roxanne on this one," Roy said. "And you can't imagine how much it pains me to say that. But it sure sounds like it's the husband. I'm not sure what he did, but I'm convinced he did it."

"Yes, but the million-dollar life insurance was for <u>him</u>, not her," Laurence Baxter offered. "The wife's was only for $500,000."

"That may well be," Roxanne said. "But I wouldn't turn my nose up at a $500,000 payout to off Roy. No offense, dear."

"None taken," Roy said with a smile. "I'd do the same for you." He squeezed her hand.

"You say he was looking through magic books while his nephews had their lesson?" Baxter asked.

I nodded. "I'm not sure if it was plural or singular, but yes, he spent all his time at the bookcase. Seated. Patiently paging through a book. Or was it two books? I wish I could remember."

"Ah yes, the legendary Harry Marks Lending Library," Roy said with a giggle. "That's one surefire way to go out of business: let your customers take the products home for free." He followed this up with another sharp laugh.

"That might be the case, but it's not a quick process, that's for sure," I offered. "He's had the store for over forty years. And it seems to work. People trust Harry. And they trust his recommendations."

"Yes," Baxter agreed. "We've had long discussions on this very topic. He explained how he would sell someone Nickels & Dimes before he'd sell them Scotch & Soda. He'd sell them a Svengali Deck before he'd ever offer them a Brainwave Deck. There was a process you had to go through to get past Harry the Gatekeeper."

"Didn't he get into a big fight with the CEO of a company or something who wanted to buy and perform some trick he'd seen a motivational speaker do?" Roxanne asked. "Or am I remembering that wrong?"

"No, you've got it. It's legendary. I was there when it happened," I said. "This guy came in, full suit, very fancy. He said, 'Do you sell the Torn and Restored Newspaper trick that I saw Lou Holtz do at a luncheon?' And Harry said, 'Sure, I sell it. But not to you.' I still remember the look on that guy's face when Harry said that."

"'Sure, I sell it. But not to you,'" Roy repeated with a cackle.

"It was quite the argument, a real blow-out. I'm surprised it didn't end up in the papers," I said.

"I can see the headlines now," Roy continued. *"Lowly Magic Dealer Slaps Down Local Bigwig."*

"But the fact is, he was right," I said. "The guy never would've been able to perform that trick properly. He would've looked like an idiot."

"Did he leave in a huff?" Roxanne asked.

"Or a minute and a huff," Roy added, doing a decent Groucho impression.

I shook my head. "I think Harry finally talked him into buying The Coloring Book trick. And the guy was ultimately thrilled—he was the hero at his event."

"A classic," Baxter agreed. "Always a crowd-pleaser and a snap to learn."

"Another ego-driven executive came in once, wanting to buy The Linking Rings. No, strike that. Not wanting. Insisting," I said.

"Harry turned him away?" Baxter asked.

"No, the guy was just a jerk and wouldn't take no for an answer. So, Harry told him he'd sell him the set of rings. But—he added—when the guy wanted to bring them back because he couldn't do the trick, Harry wasn't offering a refund."

"Let me guess: the guy couldn't, and Harry didn't," Roy said.

"That's exactly how it played out. Trust me: You don't want to get on the wrong side of Harry Marks when he's selling magic."

We were heading West on Highway 494 and I realized this was the same route that Heather Clark's phone had last taken, just about six days earlier. I looked around, wondering if there might be any clues along the highway to her disappearance. Nothing jumped out at me.

"It's the same thing with The Dancing Cane," Baxter added. "I had a client who wanted to do it as part of his speech. I told him, sir, I make it look easy. But you're not going to pick it up on a Tuesday afternoon and perform it on Tuesday night. Not successfully at least."

"Executives are the worst," Roy agreed. "Remember that woman who wanted to do your quick-change act?"

Roxanne snorted at the memory. "Oh, what a nightmare. She had seen our Vegas act and wanted us for her corporate event. But with one caveat: She wanted to perform the quick-change routine I did."

"The one you spent ten years perfecting?" Baxter asked.

"More like fifteen," Roxanne corrected. "She didn't have a clue! I finally got her to drop it when I explained that she was too skinny to make it work. That was a flat out lie, but it did the trick."

"That's the problem with our craft," Roy said, sounding strangely serious. "We make it look easy, so any idiot thinks he can do it."

This was greeted with murmurs of approval from the rest of us.

"Anyway," Baxter said. "Back to your missing persons case. I agree: If you can figure out what book or books he was reading, it might give you some insight."

"Or not," Roy said.

"Yes, or not," Baxter agreed. "But I will say this: If you wanted a lot of information on how to make something disappear, you couldn't find a better place to sit than in front of a wall of magic books."

"Here's what I want to know," Roxanne said, loudly and suddenly. "In spite of all this cloak and dagger nonsense we're going through, does Harry have any idea what's going on?"

"It's hard to tell with Harry," I said. "He's so damned inscrutable. I will say this: if we pull this off, this will be the first time in my memory that someone was able to trick Harry Marks."

And that possibility—the slim prospect of fooling Harry Marks—was the focus of our conversation on the rest of our drive.

We no longer talked about what might have happened to Heather Clark. Was she now living in Brazil somewhere? Did her sudden and mysterious disappearance involve possibly embezzled funds? Had she been kidnapped, and a ransom demand was forthcoming? Or did her husband do something nefarious?

No, the question which occupied our conversation for the next twenty minutes was this: Was it physically possible to ever actually fool Harry Marks?

5

M egan's store, Chi & Things, was packed.

The shop, which was several doors down from Chicago Magic, usually did a brisk business. But today's crowd seemed larger than usual.

I spotted Megan behind the register and snaked my way toward her.

"Busy day?"

She was just finishing a sale, handing the customer a receipt and a quick thank-you. "It sure is," Megan said as she turned to me, clearly a little out of breath. "It's probably because Franny is doing live readings today, but she'd be the first to pooh-pooh that."

I was puzzled by this. "I thought Franny only did phone readings?"

"Oh, she does," Megan said. "On special occasions, she just does them from here instead of at home. It always draws a crowd."

She gestured toward the back of the store. I spotted Franny, nestled deep within a big comfy chair. She is such a wisp of an old woman, she nearly disappeared into the ratty recliner. She was chatting animatedly into her cell phone, but she stopped long enough to give me a quick wave from across the room.

While it was by no means a full-time business, Franny had for years been making extra income as a phone psychic. Literally a phone psychic; she said her powers only worked when she was on the phone with a subject.

"So, people are calling her from their homes?" I said, still not understanding exactly what was going on.

"It's part of a store promotion, didn't I mention it to you?"

I shook my head. "I don't think so."

"Oh, well the only way to get the reading is to come into the store and call from here." She gestured to the other side of the store, where a line of people had formed. The woman at the head of the line was deep in conversation on her phone, while the others waited patiently for their turn to call Franny for a personal reading.

Harry and Franny had been together for several years now, but I was always still a bit mystified at the odd pairing: The skeptical magician and the self-employed psychic. But they seemed to make it work. People had pointed out that Megan and I had a similar dynamic, but the truth was she was less of a psychic than Franny. And I was certainly less of a magician than Harry.

"How did your airport pickup go?" Megan asked.

"Surprisingly well," I said. "Despite having to go through customs, Laurence Baxter still beat the Templetons to Baggage Claim."

"I didn't know you needed to go through Customs when you came in from Las Vegas."

I couldn't tell if she was kidding or not, so I assumed she wasn't. "No, you can still come and go pretty freely from Las Vegas. They're a bit stricter when you're coming in from London."

"You'd think it would be just the other way around; I am far more suspicious of someone traveling here from Vegas."

I couldn't find anything to disagree with in that statement.

"Did you get them into the hotel okay?" She asked this while she quickly rang up another customer's purchase.

"Yes, no problem. Roy had a lot of luggage, so that slowed us down a bit."

"You know, I still think they could've stayed with us," Megan said.

I shook my head. "Three guests in their seventies, in a two-bedroom apartment, with two people and two cats already living there? Directly across the street from Harry's two favorite hang outs? That strikes me as a recipe for disaster."

"I've got that recipe if you ever want it," came a raspy voice from behind me.

I turned to see Franny had vacated her comfy chair and was now standing beside me.

"I'm on a break," she said. "What's this about a recipe for disaster?"

"Megan and I were just discussing our decision to put our three out-of-town guests into a hotel and not turn our home into an overcrowded Airbnb."

"Oh, you're right, that would've been a recipe for disaster. That's far too close to the magic shop and the bar. Harry would know, he would just know."

"Well, he doesn't seem to know yet, as far as I can tell. You're with him every day. What do you think?"

Franny shrugged. "The man is the dictionary definition of impenetrable. However, in this instance, I think he is completely unaware of what we have planned for Sunday. Whether or not he'll like it, well, that's an entirely different issue."

"How are your calls going?" Megan asked.

"Oh, goodness, it's just one thing after another with these

people," Franny sighed. "Problem after problem after problem. I know you said Mercury is in retrograde, but I think it's more like turbo retrograde. Everyone's life seems to be both topsy and turvy. I spent the morning talking people off the ledge, again and again."

"Not literally, I hope," I said.

"Not today, thank heavens. But, oh my goodness, there's something in the ether. Speaking of which, I had a twinge about you this week."

"Oh?"

"Yes. It wasn't really sharp, couldn't quite get it in focus. You've lost something, but it's not really lost. Does that ring any bells?"

I shook my head. Franny's *twinges*—particularly about me —were often dense and opaque. "No. But I suppose if whatever it is isn't really lost, I probably don't need to worry about it."

"Good point," she said. "If you want to get on the phone with me, it might come in clearer."

I looked at the people patiently waiting in line across the room. "I think you've got your hands full."

"Indeed I do." She turned to Megan. "I'm taking a quick break. I'm going to run across the street and grab a coffee and a cruller. Be back in five."

As Franny headed toward the door, I turned back to Megan.

"Is turbo-retrograde really a thing?" I asked.

Megan shrugged. "Well, if sales in the store are any indicator, it certainly suggests people are gearing up for something. We've just about sold out on serenity candles. And the anxiety necklaces, calm strips and dream powders are jumping off the shelves. People are edgy. One woman even had a screaming fit because we're out of calming cream."

"What did you do?"

"I told her yelling never solved anything. And then I said

she could get her butt over to CVS and pick up a jar of rescue remedy. Let them deal with her."

"So much for 'The Customer is Always Right.'"

"Oh, that's never been true. You know what I mean, you deal with the public."

I looked around the crowded store. "Well, maybe, but in much smaller numbers." A thought occurred to me. "Before I forget, I told Harry I borrowed Nathan's car to transport some new shelves for your store. So, if he asks, that's why I needed it."

She looked around her shop wistfully. "Just what I need: more shelves for products I can't keep in stock."

"Speaking as a store owner who has items on his shelves that were there when I was a teenager—and will probably still be there when I'm Harry's age—please understand if I'm not super sympathetic to your impressive sales volume."

"Understood. See you tonight," Megan said. She gave me a quick kiss on the cheek before turning to the next waiting customer.

* * *

IN SHARP CONTRAST to all the activity at Chi & Things, there were no customers in Chicago Magic when I stepped through the front door a few minutes later.

Harry was seated behind the counter, paging through the latest copy of *Genii* magazine. I was suddenly struck with a feeling of *deja vu*: His posture and position were the same as when I'd worked in the store as a teenager; he was just a lot grayer and slightly more bent over, his eyes straining to read the small print.

Before I could get too caught up in the nostalgia of the moment, he looked up at me, peering over his glasses.

"So, did everything go smoothly with the transportation of your special cargo?" he asked.

The question stunned me for a moment. Was he referring to the out-of-town guests I'd just picked up at the airport? Did he know Baxter and the Templetons were in town? Was the birthday surprise already blown?

"What?" That sparkling retort was all I was able to come up with, until I suddenly recalled the ruse I'd manufactured. "Oh, the shelves. Yes, they're fine. All transported. No issues."

"All right then," he said as he lowered himself from the stool. "If you no longer need me, I'll retire to my spot next door. I suspect a few of the Mystics have already preceded me."

I glanced at my watch. It was very likely one or two of his pals were already in residence, trading quips and lies from their special table in the back of the bar."

"You're probably right," I said. "Thanks for minding the store. Oh, and thanks for the ideas on the Square Circle. It was a huge help."

"No problem, Eli. Always happy to help another magic store owner make a sale. When do you see your hapless twins next?"

I mentally flipped through my teaching schedule, which had become—thankfully—surprisingly crowded. "Tomorrow," I said. "I think."

"Well, something tells me a sale is imminent. You'll soon be seeing the last of this Square Circle illusion."

It was only later I realized Harry was both absolutely right —and dead wrong—in his prediction.

"They love it, of course. But to be honest, they're a bit on the fence. They're of two minds, which is not uncommon with this pair." She followed this up with a nervous laugh, which seemed to be something of a feature with Mrs. Claxton.

"That's no problem," I reassured her.

"They tell me they hate the idea of buying a prop just because it's intriguing, even if they know deep down it might never be a part of their act."

I smiled. "Well, that level of self-understanding immediately puts them far ahead of many magicians two or three times their age."

We looked across the shop at the two boys. They were working with the Square Circle illusion. They'd gone through the routine I'd shown them once and then switched sides and were doing it again. Although I'm sure it made some difference to them, it looked exactly the same to me.

"Thanks for doing all this work putting this routine together for them," she continued.

"Oh, no problem," I said. "It was fun. My uncle helped out, and we had a pleasurable hour or so banging around ideas."

"I hope it wasn't time wasted. I really can't tell if they're going to add this to their act or not. They often surprise me with their choices."

"Not to worry," I repeated. I was beginning to wonder why I was spending so much time reassuring this woman that it was okay not to buy the prop. "Any time I get to spend with my uncle generating magic ideas is, I think, always time well spent."

Mrs. Claxton made a non-committal affirmative sound and returned her attention to her two young sons.

She was a high-strung woman, probably somewhere in her thirties. On the handful of occasions we'd met before, she always looked like she was either coming from—or going to—the gym. Her standard weekend wardrobe appeared to be a black silk running jacket, and tights or leggings or whatever women call those things. She had long blonde hair, which she pulled back in a tight ponytail, and then covered with a baseball cap. Or maybe it was a golf cap. Whatever it was, overall I got the sense she spent a lot of effort to make herself look casually thrown together.

If I was remembering correctly, she worked at some big financial-investment-insurance-stock market sort of establishment. Something having to do with taking other people's money and making more of it, I guess. Which sounded great and always seemed like something I should look into, until I realized I didn't really <u>have</u> any money.

That wasn't entirely true. I made money from the occasional magic gig, and I'd started to make money teaching magic lessons. The store was finally not just breaking even, but actually turning a profit, albeit a small one. Plus, I felt like we were beginning to turn the corner on the bar next-door. And, of course, Megan's store was always going gangbusters, doing what Harry would call "a land office business," an expression which has never made any sense to me.

So, all in all, I figured at some point I would need to hire someone like Audrey Claxton to handle my money. That is, once I finally got some.

People with actual jobs always puzzled me. I mean, what did they do? Having never had what one might call a <u>real</u> job, I was mystified by the concept. I couldn't exactly put my finger on it, but it felt to me like everyone who had a job was a grown-up. And that somehow—now well into my thirties—I had, through luck or misfortune, avoided that step.

Yet it never really bothered me.

There's an old TV show I used to watch with Uncle Harry. It has long been off the air, but he loved it so much he bought the DVD set. It was called *Then Came Bronson* and it was about a guy—not so surprisingly named Bronson—who traveled around the country on his motorcycle, getting into new adventures every week. It was like the show *Route 66*, but with half the regular cast. Or *The Fugitive*, but without the murder and the one-armed man.

My favorite part of the show was the opening. It was a scene of Bronson pulling up at a stoplight. Next to him is a businessman in a car. The businessman looks over at the guy on the motorcycle.

"Taking a trip?"

"Yeah."

"Where to?"

"I don't know. Wherever I end up, I guess."

Long sigh from the businessman. "Man, I wish I was you."

"Really? Well, hang in there."

And then Bronson would roar off on his motorcycle.

The weird thing was—even at that young age—I completely understood where Bronson was going. He was off to an adventure. But what was the businessman going to do? The question puzzles me to this day. What do businesspeople do all day? Twenty years later and I still don't have a clear idea.

I suddenly felt like I was being rude to Mrs. Claxton, who had settled onto a stool in front of one of the counters and was scrolling through her phone.

"So, how is your brother doing?" I tentatively asked. I wasn't sure of the social protocol in this situation. But I was also curious.

"Oh, he's miserable. I think he feels totally ineffectual. I mean, what can you do? So, he sits at home and waits by the phone."

"And the police don't have any other leads?"

She shook her head. "One of them told me—confidentially —that in a missing persons case, after a certain number of days, either a body turns up or they discover the person has gone on the lam. I mean, *something* happens. But so far, nothing."

"Does that seem like something she would do? I mean, just disappear?"

Mrs. Claxton shrugged. "Heather was a hard one to read. I never quite got my bearings with that one.

"To be honest," she continued, lowering her voice, "I was never sure it was a good match, even from the beginning. Of course, they had their problems like any couple. God knows my ex and I had (and have) our own share of drama." She glanced over at the twins and then looked up at me. "You know how some couples just seem to click?"

I nodded. I certainly had seen it with Uncle Harry and Aunt Alice before she died. I saw it now with Harry and Franny. Megan and I had absolutely clicked from the moment we met. The only hindrance had been that she was in the midst of a divorce at the time. But once that obstacle had been overcome, it had been—relatively speaking—smooth sailing.

"Well, Heather and Matt never really clicked, at least in my mind," she said. "*Something* was always a little off about them. I could never put my finger on it. Matt never said anything, of course. That's not his way. But I always felt for some reason they wouldn't be one of those couples celebrating their fifty-year anniversary. Of course, which of us is?" she added with a cynical laugh. "That ship has sailed for me, that's for sure."

"I'm surprised they haven't done one of those media pleas," I said. "You know, where the spouse goes on TV and asks the public for help, maybe offers a reward for leads, that sort of thing."

"There has been talk about Matt doing that," she said. "He wanted to set up a reward right away, but the police talked him out of it for some reason. They said a reward brings all the nutcases out of the woodwork. But I still keep thinking the phone is going to ring and we'll hear from some kidnappers. Or something."

I didn't have anything to add to that notion and it looked like the boys had made it through the routine a couple of times. So, I turned my attention back to my actual students. We discussed how the process had felt and I offered a couple of minor tweaks to their handling. And then we were off to the rest of the lesson, which in this case consisted of re-thinking their Cards Across routine.

Harry had recommended I take a look at Morgan & West's version, and I had to grudgingly agree their approach was smarter, cleaner and more fooling. Plus, it was perfect for a two-person team. The remainder of the lesson was spent working on the details of that routine and no more was said of the Square Circle illusion.

After they left, I spent a few minutes disassembling the table, and then tried to decide what to do with the box and the tube. I really couldn't tell if they were going to purchase it or not. I knew one way to ensure they would buy it, however, would be to disassemble it entirely and put it back up into storage. But that struck me as being needlessly superstitious, and so I left the Square Circle illusion right there on the counter, not at all sure whether I had a sale or not.

It was really the least of my problems and I knew it. In twenty-four hours, we were going to attempt the impossible: We were going to try to surprise Harry Marks.

7

L aurence Baxter's voice cut through the wall of sound which filled the bar, as we all scrambled to finish up the final details before Harry's semi-scheduled arrival. As soon as he began to speak, everyone stopped what they were doing.

"If it be now, 'tis not to come," Baxter intoned. *"If it be not to come, it will be now. If it be not now, yet it will come—the readiness is all."*

This was followed by a hush of silence as his British accent echoed throughout the room.

"I guess that's just Shakespeare's way of saying if Harry doesn't show up, we're still going to have ourselves a wild, kickass party," Roy Templeton offered.

Baxter was the first to laugh and we all joined in.

The preceding hour had been a bit of a mad dash, exacerbated by the fact that none of us knew *exactly* when Harry would be arriving. That had been an early ground rule set by our tiny planning committee. Nothing would arouse Harry's suspicions more than making up a random event, and then telling him he had to be at a particular place at an exact time.

As Franny had said at that first, super-clandestine meeting, "Sorry kids. That dog won't hunt."

Instead, we opted to organize the event around his rather predictable schedule: He and Franny generally came by the bar on Sunday afternoons, between three and four. So, everything was structured around him sticking to this probable pattern.

"Of course," my friend Nathan had suggested at the first meeting, "there's always the slim chance that he'll pick that day to decide to stay home."

"Yes, we always run that risk with him," Franny agreed. "We've only been together a few years and I still can't always predict him. And I'm a psychic! Just when you think he's going to zig, the old coot will zag. If worse comes to worst and he refuses to come with me to the bar, I'll just drop the pretense and tell him about the surprise party. But I don't think it will come to that."

"I hope it doesn't," Megan offered. "Surprises are always so much more fun."

I wasn't one hundred percent sure Harry would agree with that statement. We would find out one way or the other in about an hour. Or less.

Although the bar was packed with people, you'd be hard pressed to recognize that as you approached the building. All of Harry's friends had been instructed to park several blocks away; not just down the street, but literally well out of sight. We all knew if Harry spotted one recognizable car which shouldn't be in front of the bar, our well-planned pretense would crumble.

On the positive side, virtually all the surviving Minneapolis Mystics had shown up. This itself was no small trick, as most of them were pushing eighty or beyond. Regulars Abe Ackerman and Gene Westlake arrived together, with Gene carrying the small case which held his ventriloquist dummy, Kenny. Hypnotist Clarence Sager, coin magician Sam Esbjornson, juggler Harold Meyer, mime Winston Moss, and spooky magician

Vince Rhodes rounded out the group. They hadn't all been together in the same location since the death of founding member Max Monarch a couple years before.

But it wasn't just performers who had gathered to honor Harry on this day. Over the years, he had amassed a truly mixed bag of friends and acquaintances, from all parts of town and all walks of life. For many of these folks, their only connection to anyone else in the room was the fact that they all knew and loved Harry Marks.

There were people from his walking club at the Mall of America, which Harry and Franny attended religiously during the snowy months. His old barber had shown up, as had the new one who replaced him. His favorite baristas from three nearby coffee shops were also in attendance. Past students of all ages were there, many demonstrating to each other the card and coin moves they'd learned from Harry.

Newer friends included a group he'd dubbed the Four Horseman of Criminal Apprehension. These were four law enforcement-related pals (including my ex-wife's husband, Homicide Detective Fred Hutton) who had—for some unknown reason—picked this bar as their post-work hangout. Deirdre and her taciturn husband had even arrived extra early to help us prepare the room.

Our out-of-town guests, Laurence Baxter and Roy and Roxanne Templeton, would be joined—via pre-recorded videos —by some well-known magicians who couldn't make the trek to Minneapolis, but wanted to offer Harry birthday congratulations. Mac King sent a very funny tribute, as did David Copperfield. Through gritted teeth I had even reached out to Morgan & West, who sent a short video that was not only hysterically funny, but also poignant and heartfelt. And, because it was Morgan & West, it was expertly produced, which for some reason bugged me even more.

Nathan and I were behind the bar, doing a final check of

supplies. Although Nathan is a world-class children's magician, over the last few months he'd also proven himself to be a first-rate magic salesperson. He had—nearly single-handedly—made the magic shop profitable for the first time in years. So, it had occurred to me he might demonstrate similar skills behind the bar. Today would be the first real test of his newly learned bartending skills, as he had volunteered to operate the open bar during the party.

"I think we're going to need more ice," I said, seeing the ice drawer was less than half full.

"I'll grab some from the back," Nathan offered. "Hey, I noticed the Square Circle illusion is still out on the counter. Have the Claxton twins decided not to add it to their act?"

"On the contrary, their mother sent me a text this afternoon," I said, closing the ice drawer. I scanned the rows of glasses, to see if any of them needed another pass in the dish washer. "They've decided they very much want to buy it. She said she would swing by and pick it up sometime this week."

"Congratulations. Great sale."

"Well, thanks, but I believe your sales stats are still ridiculously higher than mine."

"Hey, remember what you told me when I first started working the counter? *It's not all about selling. It's about meeting customer needs.*"

"Yes, well that was before I started generating regular balance sheets. So, while I appreciate that philosophy in the abstract, on a day-to-day basis, I think it really is about the selling."

Nathan chuckled as he headed into the back room, which held—among other bar necessities—a large ice machine. It was old and in need of replacement, but it would have to wait patiently in line behind more pressing purchases, of which the bar had no shortage.

I looked up to see Deirdre headed toward me, with her hulking husband in lockstep behind her.

"We're out of crêpe paper," she announced. There may have been a tone in her voice suggesting that I had somehow made a serious error in the amount of crêpe paper I'd purchased. Or it might have been judgement-free and just her natural lack of warmth shining through.

"However, in my view, I feel we have sufficiently festooned the place," she continued. The three of us looked around at all the bright yellow and orange and red and purple streamers they had hung from the ceiling. She turned to her husband. "What do you think?"

"I am without opinion," he said slowly.

Wise move, I thought to myself. Pick your battles.

Nathan's question about the Square Circle illusion had stirred a thought in my brain. "So, do you have any further news on the Heather Clark case?"

Homicide Detective Fred Hutton shook his head. "No, we're pretty much at a standstill. We're well past the first forty-eight hours, which is significant. That's the critical interval." He seemed much more interested in talking about the case than commenting on the crêpe paper situation. "It doesn't mean something won't break. But—generally—if that doesn't happen in those first couple days, it really reduces the odds of us finding her. However, I am not without hope. One of the first things you learn is statistics apply to groups, not to individuals. Best not to be too swayed by the numbers."

Deirdre looked like she had a contrary response all loaded and ready to go. But before she could offer her opinion, her phone beeped. She shifted her focus and pulled it out. She gave the screen a quick glance and then rolled her eyes.

"Another email from your pest?" her husband suggested.

"Sadly, yes."

"That's the new Assistant to the Assistant District Attorney?" I suggested. "Barry, right?"

"Barry indeed," Deirdre snapped. "He likes to give me the illusion he's working all weekend when we both know he's not. I swear to God, he writes up all these emails on Friday afternoon, and then programs his phone to send them out at different times during the weekend."

"To give the illusion he's hard at work?" I offered.

"Illusion is the right word. He wants me to think he's working his butt off. But he's not fooling me."

"An illusion which doesn't fool is a bad illusion indeed." This came from Laurence Baxter, who had sauntered up to the bar just in time to hear Deirdre's outburst. "Excuse me for interrupting," he added with a genial smile.

"Not at all," Deirdre said graciously. It always amazed me how much nicer she was to strangers. She turned to her husband. "Let's put your height to good use for once. You can help me adjust that 'Happy Birthday' banner. It's more askew than my OCD can tolerate."

He wordlessly followed her. Baxter turned to me.

"Are they married?"

"For now, yes," I said. "The over/under on that pairing shifts on a daily basis."

I don't think he quite knew what to make of that statement, so he smoothly shifted the topic. "I certainly hope Harry appreciates all the effort you and Megan have put into this celebration."

"I hope so too," I said. "I'm just trusting when he said he didn't want any fuss made about his birthday, what he actually meant was we should make some fuss about his birthday."

"All will be revealed in the next few minutes, that's for certain," Baxter said with a grin. "Tell me, is the bar open yet?"

"Our bartender has gone to wrestle some more ice from our

ice machine, but I can certainly grab you something. What would you like?"

"Is there any chance you've got a Bailey's on hand? Neat," he added.

"We do indeed." I turned to scan the multitude of bottles which made up the back wall of the bar. I finally spotted the bottle of Bailey's. I pulled it down and poured a generous serving for Baxter, who thank me profusely before he headed back into the crowd.

As I returned the bottle back to its place on the dark mahogany shelf, I wondered when was the last time anyone had ordered a Bailey's in this bar? Looking down at the ledge, I realized the answer was right in front of me: The outline of the bottom of the bottle was completely visible, defined by the dust which had gathered around it. Clearly it had been quite some time since anyone had picked up the bottle I was currently holding.

I looked at the dust again and realized my housekeeping habits in the bar were just as haphazard as the ones I had next door; the magic shop didn't need dusting as much as a good power washing.

And then I realized something else. An idea, or at the very least, the beginnings of a good notion. Figuring I would just be gone for a few seconds, I slipped through the door which connected the bar to the magic shop.

I probably should have mentioned to someone that I was leaving, but it didn't occur to me at the time. As it turned out, it was a longer—and more treacherous—trip than I initially anticipated.

* * *

THE SHOP, of course, was dark. So, my first step was to turn on the lights. I flipped the switches by the front door, but the lighting is so bad in the store that this didn't really make an appreciable difference. Like the ice machine next door, the fluorescents in the ceiling desperately needed to be updated. But that was a concern for another day.

Instead, once the lights were on, I turned my attention to the bookshelf across the room. When was the last time we'd sold a book? Was it the Tommy Wonder two-volume set after the magic club meeting the previous Monday? Had anyone browsed the bookcase since then? I wasn't sure, but hoped my lousy housekeeping habits would give me the answer.

Just like the shelf which held the Bailey's bottle, I noticed a thin layer of dust on all the bookshelf's visible surfaces. I looked at the spot where the Tommy Wonder books had been; the wood was dust free where they had sat, and the dust in front of that spot had been smeared when Nathan had removed the books from the shelf.

I scanned the shelves for a similar smear and was rewarded moments later. There was no gap in the line of books, but in one spot the dust was smeared, indicating the book behind it had been recently taken out and put back. The spine was white, which matched my vague memory of the book Matt Clark had read every time he came into the shop.

I peered closer and read the four words on the spine: "Designing Miracles. Darwin Ortiz."

I delicately pulled the book out and carried it over to the counter, where the lighting was (nominally) better. I wasn't sure what to do with the book now that I had it, but then noticed the dustjacket flap was holding a place in the back of the book. I flipped it open to reveal the designated spot: It was part of the Appendix and was labeled Darwin's Laws. What followed were twenty-seven precepts about creating magic.

I scanned through them quickly; it had been a while since I'd read the book, but in my early days it had been something of a bible for me. Darwin's thinking on the creation of magic was legendary and there were few illusions which weren't improved when filtered through his ideas. The use of the word 'miracles' in the title was not hyperbole. Knowing Matt Clark had likely been reading this book made me wonder what ideas on misdirection he might have taken from Darwin's classic manuscript.

I pulled up a stool and began to study the pages more closely. And the more I read, the more I was able to develop a pretty good theory on what had happened to Heather Clark a little over a week before. The steps in the plan were right in front of me, aided by another recent topic: Deirdre's assistant, Barry, and his weekend email habits.

I was so engrossed in my reading, I barely registered the first knock on the door. A second, more persistent knock brought me back to reality. I marked my spot in the book with the dustjacket flap and headed across the room. My mind was still connecting the ideas in the book with the known facts about the alleged crime.

I wasn't sure why someone would be knocking on the door at four o'clock on a Sunday, but figured it was probably a guest for the surprise party who hadn't read the details of the email carefully. I was prepared to direct whoever it was toward the bar next door, but froze once I swung the door open.

It was literally the last person on earth I expected to see.

It was Matt Clark.

8

"Oh good, you <u>are</u> opened," he said.

I was immediately thrown-off by his smile and upbeat attitude.

"My sister asked me to swing by at some point this week and pick up something she's buying for the twins?" he continued. "I was just driving past, saw the lights were on and thought I might be able to avoid another trip over here."

I tried to form words, but my mouth and my brain were both equally surprised by this odd turn of events. "Um, yeah, sure, no problem," I stammered. "It's right over here. Let me get it for you."

I gestured him into the store, my mind running at a million miles an hour.

I believe I had figured out—thanks to the book—the broadbrush strokes of what he had done with his wife, what he intended to do, and how he was likely to get away with it.

The key, I quickly determined, was to act like I knew none of that. Instead, I needed to give him the Square Circle illusion and send him on his way. Then rush next door to tell Deirdre and her husband what I had figured out.

And I think it might have gone that way, except for one key mistake on my part. I had left the book on the counter. Right next to the Square Circle illusion. My mind was so focused on handing him the prop pieces, I didn't immediately recognize the fateful book was right there, in plain sight.

And then I glanced at Matt Clark and saw that he too had seen the book. He looked at me and his expression said it all.

For some insane reason, I suddenly remembered an exchange from one of Harry's favorite movies, 'The Lion in Winter.' I couldn't remember the quote exactly, but it was something like, '*I know. You know I know. I know you know I know.*'

And that much was clear to me from Matt Clark's expression. He knew I knew.

He glanced down at the book again. "I don't know much about magic, but I enjoyed looking through that book the few times I was here for my nephews' lessons. There's a lot of good ideas in that book. I probably should have bought it."

"Or you could have just borrowed it," I suggested, working hard to sound casual. I gestured to the hand-written placard above the shelf and the numbers 793.8. "We call it Harry's Lending Library."

"Not sure why I picked <u>that</u> book. But I opened it up and immediately started getting ideas."

"That often happens with the best magic books."

"Imagine. I could have picked any book off this shelf. What made me pick this one? Fate?"

"Not so sure I believe in fate," I said.

"Me neither." He wasn't just being cool. He was ice cold.

In the distance, I could hear the dim sound of a group of excited people yelling, "Surprise!" This was followed by laughter and then more laughter. Harry must have arrived for his surprise party. I was sorry I had missed his entrance and wasn't feeling entirely certain I would be around for any of that afternoon's celebration. I'd never know if he was pleased or pissed about the party.

"Do you have any favorite parts?" Matt asked. "In the book?"

I turned my attention back from the bash I was missing to the possibly fatal situation in front of me. I considered his question. "Well, Darwin's ideas on Time Displacement and Spatial Distance, of course, are key," I said.

I decided at that moment to tear down any pretense between us.

"Heather's phone call from the Mall of America, for example," I continued. "I'm guessing you programmed her phone to call your phone at an appointed time?"

He paused for just a split second and then nodded. Something had clearly shifted between us, and he appeared willing to go with it. "Like many things these days, there's an app for that."

"My ex-wife's assistant uses a similar technique with emails. And I'm guessing you made sure her phone's battery was super low and stuck it on some vehicle you knew would be leaving the Mall at a specific time?"

"Garbage trucks. They have very scheduled rounds."

"Good thinking."

"Thanks."

"So, the phone is tracked leaving the Mall, and then an hour later it's not only dead, but buried under a couple of tons of garbage in a landfill somewhere."

"Most likely." He glanced down at the book again.

"So, she was never at the mall."

He nodded.

"You drove the car out there, left the keys in it, ditched the phone in a garbage truck and jogged home."

"Right on all counts."

"But honest Minnesotans let you down. No one stole the car."

"Nope. But as primary elements go, that was a *nice to have*, not a *need to have*. Anything else?"

"Just about everything else," I said, my mind still racing. "Darwin Ortiz literally wrote the book on misdirection. Like, 'Make the important seem unimportant and the unimportant seem important.' The life insurance is a perfect example of that idea put into practice: No one is going to flinch at your $500,000 payout for her death after they find out she would have gotten twice as much—a million dollars—when you died. It seemed more likely she would kill you, not vice versa."

"It's a simple idea, but clearly effective. Once they knew that, they never mentioned the insurance angle again."

"But you'll still collect a half-million dollars if—when—she dies."

"As long as I'm not the murderer, you bet. And I'm not a murderer. Not yet at least."

He chose that moment to pull a small pistol out of his pocket. He pointed it casually in my direction. Despite this new threat, his words were zinging around my brain.

Suddenly Franny's odd prediction made sense: It wasn't that something I'd *lost* wasn't really *lost*. It was something that was *missing* wasn't really *missing*. And I remembered Darwin's Law Number Seven: If you mislead the audience about <u>when</u> it happened, they will never figure out <u>how</u> it happened.

"She's not missing," I said, blurting out the words before I considered their consequences. This was a too-frequent fault I suddenly realized I might never get the chance to fix someday. "She's in the one place the police would never think to look: Your house. You've trapped her in your house. And you're going to kill her later. You're just waiting."

"Waiting," he repeated. "Like Max Malini."

Of course, he knew about Malini. Of all the magicians out

there, Malini was the most famous for his legendary patience. A magician once asked him, *"Max, how do you do the secret move without anyone seeing?"*

"You vait," he replied in his thick German accent.

"How long?"

"You vait a veek if you must!"

"So, you're just waiting," I said. "You'll get past the critical interval and then her freshly murdered body will turn up somewhere. And you will doubtlessly have an airtight alibi."

"Without a doubt. You seem to have put this all together quite nicely."

I was oddly pleased by his compliment.

And then I realized—too late, of course—that I hadn't mentioned to anyone at the party where I was headed. No one knew where I had gone, why I had gone there, what I was doing and who I might be meeting. If I disappeared or died, there would be nothing tying that act to Matt Clark. No one would know I had figured it out. No one would be busting down his basement door to rescue his wife. And certainly no one would be rescuing me.

Escaping this situation was entirely up to me and whatever wits I could muster. And I knew all too well how that had worked for me—or not—in the past.

"I think what we need to do here is create a robbery scenario," Matt Clark said. He had clearly been doing some quick thinking of his own. "You were alone in the store, someone came in, made you give them all the money in the till, and then—tragically—you were shot during the exchange. I think that will play."

I realized the scenario he was painting wasn't completely implausible. I had almost been robbed in a similar fashion a couple years back. I was hoping this story might end as nicely as that one had, but I wasn't feeling confident.

He glanced around the shop. "No CCTV cameras. Nothing

to tie me here. Any prints I may have left could have been from the many times I've been here before. So, let's make it a robbery."

He gestured with the gun that I should open the cash register. My options seemed severely limited, so I did just that. I punched a couple of keys and the register's squeaky drawer reluctantly slid open.

I was greeted with a sad cash drawer. Nowadays, most sales in the magic store, when they happen, are handled with credit cards. However, we always kept at least some cash in the drawer, for the occasional Luddite who insisted on making their purchase the old fashion way. Or, more often, for guys who didn't want the purchase to show up on their credit card statement. For more than one hobbyist magician, this is the best trick in their repertoire: buying tricks with cash to keep their spouse in the dark as to how much was being spent each month on magic props.

The amount of cash I pulled out of the drawer was not significant. In fact, I would call it meager. But the empty cash drawer would definitely give the impression we'd been robbed. With the cash in hand, I looked at the open drawer for another second. And an idea occurred to me.

I thought of something my Aunt Alice used to always say: "You bake with the flour you have."

At the same instant, I remembered what my uncle Harry had taught me over the years: truly great magicians will, from time to time, take risks on stage. A risk that something will not work. His theory was that if a miracle did happen, it would be that much more amazing. If not, you simply segued into your next trick, with the knowledge the audience would quickly forget about the failed attempt.

I looked down at the drawer. It was a longshot, but what did I have to lose? It was a risk worth taking. It was the only flour I had.

I gave the drawer one solid push, slamming it shut forcefully.

And the fates smile down on me.

Across the room, on the Gag & Gift shelf, the chattering teeth began to chatter. Loudly and suddenly. It wasn't an earth-shattering sound, but it was just the distraction I was looking for.

Matt Clark spun his head toward the sudden noise. And as he did, I picked up the only weapon available to me on the counter: The Darwin Ortiz book.

With one quick move, I grabbed the volume and swung it like a cudgel, smacking his gun hand with his much force as I could muster.

The gun sailed out of his hand. Just as it hit the floor, it went off. The sound of the bullet discharging was much louder than I had anticipated. But as luck would have it, the deadly missile came nowhere near me. I found out later it had gone through one of the many posters that lined the walls of the magic shop. Ironically, it was a poster of a magician—The Great Hermann—performing The Bullet Catch.

Matt looked over, trying to determine where the gun had landed. While he did that, I picked up the closest thing to a weapon I could find other than the book: The tube from the Square Circle illusion. Although it was made of metal, it was a lightweight metal, and I wasn't sure how much damage it would inflict. However, for the moment he no longer had a weapon, and I at least had something.

As he turned his head back toward me, I smacked him as hard as I could across the side of his face with the tube. I don't want to reveal anything about the workings of the trick, but let's just say the tube was in its heaviest phase at that point. So it carried more heft than it might have had. And even then—on impact—it immediately caved-in a bit on one side. The tube that is, not his face.

I realized, briefly, if I was indeed selling this trick to the Claxton twins, I would need to order a replacement tube at some point. But that was not my biggest concern at the moment.

For his part, Matt looked dazed, which had been one of my key goals. My primary objective had been to make him unconscious, but under the circumstances I was willing to live with dazed.

I quickly assessed my situation. I was behind the counter and he was in front of it, so at least we had that physical space between us. I could turn and run through the curtains into the back room, but that would give him time to pick up the gun and follow me. With the weapon in hand, he wouldn't have to get very close to kill me. So, any small distance I might be able to put between us probably wouldn't matter.

I looked to other options.

I considered making a dive for the gun, but it was closer to him than it was to me. And he was bigger than me. If this turned into a hand-to-hand contest, my money wasn't on me. So that didn't seem like a good idea.

I remembered that Uncle Harry had once successfully defended himself in the store, using only a single can of fart spray. However, that product—versatile as it may be—was currently on the other side of the store and not within my reach.

I looked at the bent tube in my hand and glanced at its partner: the square wooden box, with its fancy painted exterior. Well, as my Uncle Harry would say, "In for a penny."

I grabbed the wooden box and swung it in a wide arc. It connected squarely with Matt Clark's head. I heard a tremendous crack. This time, I wasn't sure if it was the improvised weapon or its intended target which had produced the sickening sound.

Luckily, as it turned out, it was his head.

Matt Clark collapsed to the floor as I set the unbroken box on the counter. He was out cold. The box looked untouched. I made a mental note to include the prop's obviously sturdy construction as part of any future sales pitch for the Square Circle.

The sound of the gunshot had definitely been heard in the bar next door. And, as luck would have it, there were more than a few people at the party who were trained in the tactic of running <u>toward</u> a gunshot and not away from it.

This cavalry—Homicide Detective Fred Hutton and his pals —burst through the door just a few seconds after Matt Clark hit the floor.

9

The party had long since ended and all that lingered were the memories and a few decorative remnants. The streamers still hung from the ceiling, waving lazily in the breeze of the weak air conditioning, yet another appliance on my ever-growing list for imminent replacement. The "Happy Birthday" sign was still askew, but it now dipped awkwardly to the left and not the right.

We also still had plenty of catered food left over, brought in from three of Harry's favorite restaurants. It was an odd mélange of Greek, Mexican and Thai food. All the guests had eaten their fill, but it looked like the remaining partygoers would be lugging home enough leftovers to cover their dinners for the rest of the week.

The crowd had thinned down to just Harry and Franny, our three out-of-town guests, and Nathan, Megan, and me.

"So, you're saying this fellow used Darwin's book as a sort of recipe for murder?" Baxter said.

"It appears that way," I replied. "Apparently, the ideas in the book about misdirection apply to more than just magic."

"I guess that means there's a whole new market and income

stream for that book now," Roy Templeton added. "Nice bonus for Darwin."

"I don't think that's what he intended when he wrote it," Harry said. "But Eli is right. Misdirection is misdirection. The basic principles are the same, whether you're trying to load an orange into your chop cup routine—"

"—or routinely chopping up your wife and loading her into the trunk of your Chevy," Roy said, completing Harry's thought.

"And to think a woman's life has been saved—due primarily to your robust and steadfast refusal to dust," Roxanne said.

"Eli's going to win a joint award from Good Housekeeping and the cops," Roy said. "And the magic store will be placed on the FBI's Ten-Most Grubby list."

"But the police found the wife and she's okay, right?" Franny asked.

I nodded. "Yes, Deirdre called right after they took him in. Matt Clark had Heather tied up in the basement, just waiting to execute the final step in his plan."

"Execute indeed," Baxter murmured.

"I'd call him a little weasel," Roy Templeton said. "But I think that would be a disservice to weasels everywhere."

"It will be interesting to see if they introduce the book into evidence at the trial," Baxter said.

"Unless he wisely pleads guilty and saves the state the money it'll take to easily prove him guilty," Harry said.

"Usually with an ego like that, they want to drag it out all the way to the end," Franny said. "All my true-crime documentaries on Netflix go on and on, with appeal after appeal."

"Nothing appealing about that guy," Roy quipped. "Eli, you should have hit him harder."

"I hate to admit it, but all in all, it was a pretty clever little plan he came up with," Baxter said. "His use of time misdirection, including backward time misdirection. That's something a lot of magicians could learn from."

"You mean for their acts, right?" Roy interjected. "Not for murdering their spouses."

"I don't know," Roxanne said slowly. "I can envision some useful applications in just about all areas."

Roy turned to Roxanne, to make sure she was kidding. She gave him an impenetrable look and took another sip of her drink, a blood-red daiquiri.

"So, Harry, were you surprised? Did we fool you?" Megan asked once the laughter had subsided.

All of us turned to Harry, who looked up from his ginger ale. His eyes twinkled.

"Which answer would make you the happiest? That you fooled me? Or that you didn't?"

"I think we did a pretty good job of covering our tracks," I offered.

"Indeed, indeed," Harry said. "A very skillful ploy on all levels."

"You had no flipping idea," Franny snapped. "We bamboozled you."

"That may well be the case. But the truth is, you'll never know," Harry said. "There were several possible clues along the way. Like Eli borrowing Nathan's car. Franny putting on lipstick today. An early delivery of a birthday card—and in person no less."

"I knew it!" I nearly shouted. "I knew it. I told her that would give it away."

"Oh, Eli," Harry said reassuringly. "It's never just one thing. It's always a culmination, a variety of factors, which leads one to be suspicious."

"Here's the thing that really bothers me," Franny said. "Getting back to the creep that Eli conked with that trick: I can see, in a fit of passion, someone lashes out. There's violence. It was never intended but it happened.

"But this guy," she continued, shaking her head. "To meticulously plan this scenario, and to keep his wife tied up in the basement with the idea of killing her. That strikes me as beyond psychopathic. He's a whole other level of monster."

"You're right," Roy agreed. "Charles Manson would have looked at this case and said, 'Whoa man, have some humanity.'"

"Well, there was at least one good thing to come out of this debacle," Harry said. He raised his glass. "Let us toast Eli."

"For the swell party?" Franny said.

"Well, yes of course," Harry conceded. "But also for a significant accomplishment within the magic community. Although it's been around for goodness knows how long, Eli may have created a completely new and unique presentation for the Square Circle. Kudos for that."

"It's a knock-out, that's for sure," Roy added.

"Yes," I said. "I think I may even have a new closer for my act. If I don't mind the occasional felony assault charge."

The evening continued in this vein for longer than any of us expected. And I think I can safely say a good time was had by all.

And as for the biggest mystery? Was Harry surprised?

The truth is, we'll never know for sure.

THE PROFESSOR'S NIGHTMARE

"And hast thou slain the Jabberwock?
    Come to my arms, my beamish boy!"
    —Lewis Carroll, Jabberwolky

1

"**O**ld people give me the willies."
         This would be an odd statement coming from just about anyone. That it had been uttered by a senior citizen—my Uncle Harry—made it all the more bizarre. And the fact that he'd declared this notion in the middle of a room filled with actual old people was just icing on the cake.

"I don't want to upset your apple cart," I said quietly. "But a large percentage of the population would consider you to be on the far side of elderly."

"I suppose that's true," Harry said.

"And we are also in the midst of the very folks of which you speak. So, you might want to keep your voice down."

"Not to worry. They're old. They probably can't even hear me."

"That's ageist," I said.

"What's that?" Harry replied, dramatically cupping his hand to his ear. He chuckled at his alleged joke and then continued. "Oh, Eli, you know I have no problem with old folks on an individual basis. In fact, I'm happy to report that some of my best friends are senior citizens. It's just when you put them together in a flock. A group. A murder. That's when I really start to get creeped out. It probably has to do with the siren song of death being louder when you start to get closer to the end of the line. I think that's why they give me the willies."

"Well, buckle up," was all I offered in reply. Because it was clear we were about to be inundated with old people.

We were just beginning our guided tour of the Lakeview Haven Senior Retreat—the four of us: Harry, his wife Franny, me, and my wife, Megan. And I suspected we would be encountering very few people—apart from the staff—south of sixty for the next hour or so.

The Lakeview Haven Senior Retreat was an impressive place. The buildings were large and modern; they had clearly been renovated within the past few years to provide seniors with comfortable accommodations and plenty of amenities.

"And what's the deal with the name of this place," Harry continued. "Lakeview Haven? A haven from what? And what lake? What view? We're not within sight of one of our state's alleged ten thousand lakes. We are, in fact, a stone's throw from a river."

I nodded patiently. I recognized we appeared to be far from even the tiniest of the state's lakes. As to which river Harry was referring to, your guess is as good as mine. Or probably better.

As a resident of the Twin Cities, you often find yourself crossing a river to get from one city to the other. In most cases, it's the mighty Mississippi. In others, it's the somewhat less mighty Minnesota River. We were close enough to old Fort Snelling, where the two rivers meet, that the body of water Harry had mentioned could easily have been either one.

But, as Harry had pointed out, regardless of which river it was, this place did not actually afford a lake view of any kind.

I filed the question of the facility's name away for a more opportune time because our host—as the saying goes—was otherwise engaged and not available for questions. At the moment, our tour guide, Samantha, was in deep conversation with Franny.

Samantha was in her fifties and wore a neat suit with her hair pinned back. She had an easy smile, and a friendly demeanor. I could tell from the way she spoke to us that she was a veteran salesperson—she didn't miss a beat as she outlined all of the amenities and services offered at Lakeview Haven. She had introduced herself as the Director of Sales and her business card identified her as being a fully qualified Realtor.

And she was very excited to meet us because, apparently, Franny was something of a rock star celebrity among the staff of Lakeview Haven.

"Your name has been on the Waiting List since I started," Samantha had gushed after introductions were made. "In fact, they tell me you've been on the Waiting List longer than anyone. Ever."

"Well, my first husband—Eugene—signed us up on that list over twenty-five years ago," Franny explained. "But every time a space opened up, I just wasn't in the mood to pack up and move. So, I'd pass." She turned to me. "You and Megan should get on the Waiting List. It doesn't cost anything to pass. They just move you down the list."

"Yes, but there is a cost to getting on the list," Megan said. "I looked on the website. It's $3,000 to join the Waiting List here."

"Really? It was only $500 when Eugene signed us up," Franny said. Her face lit up as a thought occurred to her. "Five hundred bucks and now it's three thousand? This just might be the best investment the old fool ever made."

* * *

THE DECISION TO make the move from their small suburban house to living quarters which required less weather-related maintenance had been a long time coming.

After their wedding, Harry and Franny had decided that between their two residences—his apartment above the magic shop and her house a couple miles away—it made the most sense to settle into Franny's house as their primary residence.

While the apartment over the store required virtually no outside maintenance—no shoveling, no raking, no lawn care—it also involved climbing a vertiginous set of stairs to get in or out of the place. And that mountain goat climb simply became too much for Harry to deal with on a daily basis.

So instead, they'd invested in some remodeling of Franny's story-and-a-half rambler, making it possible to live entirely on one floor of the house. The master bedroom was moved to the main floor. And a washer/dryer unit had been installed in the kitchen (a feature Franny had spotted on several of her favorite British detective shows and was excited to adopt). So, no more trips to the basement to do laundry.

The internet made it possible for groceries and all other purchases to be made on-line and delivered right to their doorstep.

As a result, they never had to step outside if they didn't want to.

"Which is the problem," Harry had grumbled one night at Mystics, the bar I owned next to the magic shop. "Without this bar to go to, we'd never get out of the house. It suits me fine, though; this establishment has always been the center of my social circle."

To illustrate, he gestured toward the other old magicians and variety acts around us. The bar had become—as I'd hoped —a meeting place for these outcast performers, many of whom had become new friends.

There was Talia, the acrobat, who made a point of ordering

every drink "with a twist." Dan, the fire-breather, who never touched alcohol ("I swallow enough on a daily basis at my job. I leave work at work."). And then there were the others who no one could quite seem to categorize—the living statue, the contortionist, and more. All of them drawn here like moths to a flame under the twinkle of the neon sign outside which read 'Mystics' in bright blue letters.

"But poor Franny spends her days listening to me yammer on and on as she putters around the house with nothing to do. Many of her long-time friends are gone. Neither of us drive anymore. We need to find her a new social circle."

While they had explored many and varied options, this tour of Lakeview Haven Senior Retreat was the first time they'd invited Megan and me to join them. This fact alone suggested they might be serious about making a move.

"So, this isn't really just a bunch of condo apartments?" Megan asked as we made our way through the building's brightly lit, window-filled atrium.

At the far end of the atrium, we saw a grand piano surrounded by cushioned couches and armchairs, where several people were gathered for an afternoon musical performance.

"No, Lakeview Haven is a housing cooperative; it's not the same as owning a condominium in a retirement community. In a condo, each person owns their unit and a portion of the common areas," Samantha explained. "But in a co-op, we're all shareholders of the corporation that owns and manages it all. We then have the right to occupy our specific units."

"So, the units aren't condos?" Megan asked. I was glad she was pursuing this; I was having my own trouble grasping the concept.

"Nope," Samantha said with a big smile. "Condo owners own everything in their unit, while co-op owners only own personal belongings and appliances. The cooperative covers repairs for shared items like plumbing and flooring."

"So, who's in charge then?" Harry asked.

"To govern the cooperative, our members elect a Board of Directors, which in turn elects a president. This board, along with the Manager, hires and supervises the professional staff responsible for the co-op's day-to-day operations. People like me," Samantha added with a laugh.

"Of the people, by the people and for the people?" Harry suggested.

"That's Lakeview Haven in a nutshell," Samantha agreed.

"Lenin would be proud," Harry grumbled quietly to me.

"Lenin couldn't afford to get on the waiting list," I said.

"Good point."

* * *

WE LEFT the atrium and began exploring the other amenities on offer. We passed an art gallery filled with paintings, sculptures, photographs and more.

"Most of these works were done by members of Lakeview Haven," Samantha explained. "There's a lot of creativity on tap between these walls."

We continued down the hall toward the next set of doors.

"Our members love to read," Samantha continued. "And if you're like them, you'll find no shortage of great books to pore over in this room."

Throughout the tour, I had gotten the sense our guide was parroting a sales brochure, adding a light laugh at the end of each cliched phrase.

We'd followed her into what was obviously the library, which was filled with tall, oak bookshelves that reached to the ceiling and spanned wall to wall. A grand marble fireplace adorned one wall, while several plush sofas and armchairs were arranged throughout the room along with various tables and desks. At several table sat groups of people reading or conversing in quiet voices.

"If you love mysteries—which is our members' favorite genre—you'll find volumes by all the masters here: P.D. James, Daphne du Maurier, Dashiell Hammett, Ruth Rendell, Barbara Thomas, Dorothy Sayers. And, of course, local heroes like Clifford Thomas and John Sanford. Not to mention the grand dame of the genre—"

"Agatha Christie," Franny interjected. "I've read them all, dear. Back to front and cover to cover."

"Well, I'm still working my way through them, so no spoilers, okay?" Samantha said. "But I always say, if I was going to commit a murder, this is where I'd start."

"If I was going to commit a murder, I wouldn't go around announcing it," Harry grumbled. But I don't think Samantha heard him. She was already onto the next item on her well memorized spiel.

"Say, who'd like a little snack?" she said with way too much enthusiasm. The question must have been a rhetorical one, for she was already out the door and headed toward her next destination.

THE TOUR HAD BEEN SCHEDULED to coincide with lunch service at the in-house restaurant, which occupied a large corner of the complex's first floor.

A table for five had been reserved and Samantha ushered us to our seats, continuing her well-practiced sales pitch, which concerned all the other amenities found at Lakeview Haven.

"Our members love the convenience of our one-stop shopping," she said. "No need to leave the grounds for entertainment, health care, or anything else—it's all here at Lakeview

Haven. Our concierge service will help you make appointments as needed. And don't worry about your safety—we offer a secure environment with 24-hour security staff patrolling the grounds day and night. You can truly enjoy your retirement here at Lakeview Haven!"

"Sounds like you've got all the bases covered," Franny offered as she looked around the large dining room.

It was a bright, spacious room with large windows that let in plenty of natural light. A wide central aisle ran through the room, flanked by smaller tables on either side. Most of the tables were filled with elderly couples and groups of seniors happily enjoying their meals. The tablecloths were starched white linen, set off by crisp napkins folded into neat triangles.

"And here's our biggest and best secret weapon," Samantha said, pointing toward the door to the kitchen: "Our own Chef Anton!"

Right on cue, Chef Anton stepped through the swinging doors which led into the kitchen. He was a tall man with a broad build and a thick mustache.

He must have been through this dog-and-pony show many times before, because he made a beeline to Franny and Harry. It wasn't as if Megan and I were invisible; we just weren't his target audience.

He greeted the older couple warmly and then began to talk about his culinary philosophy.

"My cooking is rooted in freshness and quality, using only the best ingredients sourced locally," he said. His accent was just this side of French; not overpowering, but more like an affectation. "I also use herbs and vegetables grown right here in the center's garden whenever possible. And trust me: I can create delicious dishes for every dietary preference from vegan to kosher." He paused for effect before adding, "And I guarantee you won't be disappointed—all my meals are cooked with love!"

Harry and Franny exchanged a look.

"After years of cooking our own meals, it would be swell to have someone else cooking for us!" Franny said. "It's like we died and went to heaven."

Chef Anton chuckled in response, wagging a finger in her direction. "No, don't say that. No one dies on my watch," he said. "Now let's enjoy some delicious food! Tell me, what can I make for you today?"

After consulting the surprisingly extensive menu, I ordered the grilled salmon with a side of roasted vegetables, while Megan opted for a vegetarian quinoa bowl. Franny and Harry decided to each try the chef's special: a succulent beef tenderloin served over creamy mashed potatoes.

My grilled salmon was absolutely incredible and—judging by the oohs, aah, and cleaned plates—the rest of my dining companions enjoyed first-class meals. When we all finished our raspberry-topped chocolate mousse desserts, we had huge, satisfied smiles on our faces.

"That was absolutely delicious," Franny said with a contented sigh. "You're right, Samantha—Chef Anton is definitely your secret weapon!"

Franny glanced at Harry, her eyes gleaming. "Just think of it: No more struggling to make dinner every night!"

Harry smiled and agreed. "Yes indeed! Just imagine it: snapping our fingers and having delicious meals on the table like magic! That's a trick I'd never get tired of seeing."

Franny nodded in agreement. "This is paradise."

"Speaking of paradise, why don't we take a quick tour of the garden," Samantha said as she set her napkin down and began to stand.

Harry and I each simultaneously reached for our respective wallets, but Samantha waved it away. "Oh, no need for that," she said with a smile. "It's all on the house. Consider it a perk of the tour."

"Sounds like a drug dealer to me," Harry grumbled quietly

as we got up from the table. "The first taste is always free. That's how they get you."

"I think it's working on Franny," I replied. She was already back in deep conversation with our host.

"I think it is," Harry agreed. "The problem is, it's also starting to work on me."

* * *

WE FOLLOWED Samantha out of the restaurant and into the atrium past the Concierge Desk.

"While we're here, let me introduce you to our head concierge," Samantha said. She gestured to a sharply dressed middle-aged man wearing thick glasses. He stepped out from behind the Concierge Desk and immediately shrunk down three inches; he must have been standing on a box behind the desk.

"This is Mr. Martinson," Samantha said.

"Call me Big Steve," he said with a grin. "That's sort of my nickname around here."

"I'm sure there's a story behind that," Harry said as he shook the man's hand.

"There is indeed. We used to have another Steve who was shorter than myself, if you can believe that. To help keep us straight, one of the residents called me Big Steve."

"And presumably the other was called Little Steve?" Harry suggested.

"Oddly enough, no. They called him The Other Steve," the concierge said with a laugh. "We don't stand on ceremony and the name just stuck. I hope you enjoy your tour and decide to join us here at Lakeview Haven."

"We're leaning that way already," Franny said as she playfully nudged Harry.

"Well, this next part of the tour might tip you over entirely,"

Samantha said, segueing us cleanly into her next stop. "Let's take a look at the gardens."

THE TOUR CONTINUED across the cobblestone patio, which included a small fountain. Surrounding the patio area was a large and expansive garden, with vibrant flowers blossoming all around.

As we strolled along the stone path, Samantha pointed out the different types of herbs that Chef Anton used in his cooking, such as rosemary, thyme, sage, and basil. There were also various types of peppers—from jalapenos to habaneros—as well as tomatoes, onions, garlic, carrots, and lettuce.

But there was more to the garden than just herbs and vegetables. As we rounded a corner, I noticed an elderly man kneeling in the soil, meticulously tending to a huge and impressive bed of flowers.

"This is Mikos!" Samantha explained. "He's been taking care of this garden since Lakeview Haven opened—he knows it like the back of his hand."

Mikos looked up from his work and nodded at us with a polite smile. His grey hair and wrinkled face suggested years spent outdoors working in the sun, but his eyes were full of life.

"You must take immense pride in working this garden for so many years," Franny said. "And it shows. I don't know how you do it."

"Well, I do have some help," he said with a sad shake of his head.

Behind Mikos we could see three older women who were carefully inspecting different plants around the garden. They weren't actually working. They appeared to be taking critical notes and exchanging whispered comments.

"Ah, excellent—the Spring Sisters are back again," Samantha said, a hint of sarcasm in her voice. She led us toward the three women. "Franny, Harry—let me introduce you to three long-time Lakeview Haven residents: April, Mae and June. The Spring Sisters."

The women spun around slowly and suspiciously. They looked up at us with raised eyebrows and their lips were pursed in stern expressions. They didn't seem happy to see us. Although they weren't dressed identically, they all seemed to favor black or dark gray clothing.

The one on the left, who I assumed was April, stepped forward gruffly and welcomed us with a curt nod.

"We're not related," she said gruffly. "And we don't like nicknames."

"Yes, of course," Samantha said. "Do you want to show these potential guests around the garden?"

"Sure, I'll give you the nickel tour" she said expressionlessly, before gesturing for Franny and Harry to follow her. Mae and June brought up the rear, scowling as they followed.

April then began to give her own dour tour of the garden, making it sound like they had overseen the landscaping personally.

Megan and I hung back as Mikos returned to his weeding.

"It really is a lovely garden," Megan offered. "You've done wonders."

"Thank you. It matters not to me who gets the credit for my work. I know what side of the bread to put my butter," he explained with a knowing smile. "But for these lovely ladies, I am happy to do my work," he said as he gestured at the flowers right in front of him: tall plants with glossy leaves and deep red berries. "They grow and bloom for me and make it all worth the while."

Samantha, who had retreated from the group to scan her

phone, glanced up to see her tour group was now seemingly dispersing throughout the large garden.

"Let's move onto our final stop," she said, trying to sound loud but not too bossy. "Let's all go take a peek at Harry and Franny's apartment."

* * *

WE ALL MADE our way back to the building, walking in a line through the atrium and down a maze of hallways.

As we went, I noticed a few senior citizens here and there, sitting in chairs or walking with canes. Most of them gave us friendly smiles as we passed by, while others simply nodded their head in recognition. I'm not sure what they were recognizing. Maybe the fact that half of our group was about their same age.

But what really caught my eye as we made our way to Harry and Franny's apartment were the doors to the different apartments. A few of them were plain and colorless, but others had been personalized with artwork or small stands with flowers and plants. Some, I noticed, even had little decorative knick-knacks attached like wind chimes or sculptures of animals. Each door was a reflection of its inhabitant—each one spoke volumes about the person who lived behind it.

Finally, we reached Harry and Franny's door, which was bare save for a colorful, hand-painted sign that read: "Harry and Franny -- Welcome to Your New Home." It appeared to have been signed by many of the staff members of Lakeview Haven.

We all paused to take in the moment before Samantha took out a small key ring and opened the door to what might soon be Harry and Franny's new living space.

Harry broke the tension with a quip. "Well," he said, "Let's see what awaits us behind Door Number One."

Franny rolled her eyes and nudged him with her elbow.

As we stepped inside, the first thing which caught my eye was a large empty living room with gleaming hardwood floors. On the far side of the room were tall French doors. They were open and I could see a patio and the gardens beyond.

Franny immediately got busy considering what furniture would fit and what would have to go, while Harry started pacing off the different rooms in preparation for all their moving boxes.

I just stood there taking it all in—the large open space, the natural light from the windows, and the feeling of being welcomed into someone else's home. It felt good; it felt right.

I turned to Megan.

"Maybe we <u>should</u> get ourselves on the Waiting List," I suggested.

"Maybe we should," Megan whispered back. "It's weird, but I'm suddenly looking forward to turning fifty-five."

But before either of us could say another word, there was a sudden interruption from the patio. A small, barking dog ran in through the open French doors, followed by a tall gentleman wearing an old-fashioned tweed coat and a bow tie.

He had a full head of white hair, bright blue eyes, and a kind smile that lit up his whole face.

"Cerberus, Cerberus, stop that," the man said, shambling toward the dog, which snaked between our legs, enjoying this impromptu game of tag. Throughout it all, the dog continued to bark, shifting into a squeakier version when Samantha finally snagged the wiggling ball of fur and picked him up.

"So sorry about that," the man said with a nod to our small group. "Cerberus doesn't take to strangers, which—despite his size—makes him an ideal watchdog for someone who lives alone. Not to worry; once he gets to know you, the barking ceases. For people he knows, the most you'll get out of him will be an enthusiastic tail wag."

"Franny, Harry, this is Dr. Charles Pemberton," Samantha explained as she handed off the dog to the older gentleman. "He lives next door. He's a professor of Philosophy at the University."

"Emeritus," Pemberton added quickly. "Massively emeritus, to be honest."

"It's a pleasure to meet you, Professor," Harry said as he extended his hand.

"Oh, honorifics are unnecessary," Pemberton said with a light chuckle as he shook Harry's hand. "I have long since retired from teaching. Yet I remain keen to retain the title of 'Doctor' for its helpfulness in securing more desirable tables at restaurants. So, has Samantha presented a convincing case? Will you be joining us here at the always delightful Lakeview Haven?"

Harry and Franny exchanged a long, questioning look.

"Well, you're the psychic," Harry said quietly. "Is Lakeview Haven in our future?"

"You know," Franny said as she broke into a large grin. "I think it just might be."

2

"**D**id you know there is dust on top of dust in some spots here?" Nathan said slowly. "I never realized that dust could have stratas."

"Just think of it as dust with depth," I offered.

"Or, as Pigpen suggests in *A Charlie Brown Christmas*, it might be the soil of some great past civilization. Maybe the soil of ancient Babylon," Nathan offered.

"I know it's been a while since I cleaned in here, but it hasn't been <u>that</u> long," I said. Although, to be honest, Nathan wasn't far off. I couldn't remember the last time I'd cleaned the magic shop in any significant way.

I was making lazy circles around the store, trying to figure out where to start today's massive cleaning project. There was a lot to choose from. There were shelves and shelves of magic tricks, from simple card tricks to more complicated, multi-colored props. However, a slight glaze of dust had taken some of the shimmer off the colors.

The bookcases were stuffed side-to-side and top-to-bottom with books of various shapes and sizes. And a dust population all its own.

It was because of the dust I'd spotted on those shelves that I'd decided a thorough cleaning of the shop was required—what Franny had called a Swedish Death Cleanse.

It sounded a lot more intriguing than it turned out to be.

Franny had explained that the Swedish Death Cleanse was a deep cleaning, one that required moving and dusting every inch of the shop. It would take days, and it was going to be hard work. But it had to be done—the shop needed a fresh start.

While I worked on the bookcases—taking all the books off a shelf, dusting them individually and then giving each empty shelf a thorough cleaning—Nathan turned his attention to the display cases. While the objects inside had acquired only a small degree of personal dustiness, it was the glass on the top and the sides that really needed some serious cleaning and polishing.

To help pass the time, I'd brought out a Bluetooth speaker and sorted through my phone until I'd found the podcast I was looking for.

"Uncle Harry was a guest this week on the Lakeview Haven in-house podcast," I explained as I adjusted the volume on the small speaker.

"I thought Harry hated doing podcasts."

"Oh, he still does. Don't ever get him started on that topic. But I think Franny made him do it. To help integrate them into the community is what she said. But in reality, I think she just wanted to get him out of the apartment for a half an hour so she could finish unpacking."

"How are they settling in?"

"Franny loves it. But for Harry, the jury is still deeply sequestered."

"Well, you know how old people freak him out."

"I do indeed," I said.

Before I could add to that thought, the speaker came to life with the sound of a young, female voice. Her introduction was neatly mixed atop the opening theme music.

"Hello and welcome to episode 193 of *SWA: Seniors With Attitude, The Lakeview Haven Podcast*. I'm your host Claire Michaels, the center's Program Director. Today I'm joined by one of our newer residents: magician Harry Marks. Welcome to the show, Harry!"

"Thank you, Claire, it's great to be here," Harry said with forced cheer.

"Liar," I muttered quietly.

"So, Harry, word on the street is that you're new to the Lakeview community. How are you finding it so far?"

"It's... interesting," Harry replied with a slight laugh. "I haven't been here long, but already I can see that this community has a unique culture all its own. It's quite different from the life I was used to." He paused for a moment, as if searching for the right words. "It's definitely been an adjustment, but I'm sure if I give it some time, I'll find my place here, too."

"I understand you made your career as a professional magician."

"I did indeed."

"Can you tell us a bit about that? What shows did you appear on, where did you travel with your act, and who was your favorite audience?"

Harry chuckled. "My career has taken me to some interesting places. I started out in the 1950s as an amateur magician, performing at small venues in my hometown. The Elks, Knights of Columbus, that sort of thing.

"But over time I built a reputation for myself and before long, I was getting invitations to perform at larger venues. Before I knew it, I began to travel around the country. Then I was a regular on a popular TV show, *Magic Hour*, which put me in front of a much wider audience.

"From there I was lucky enough to make an appearance

on *The Ed Sullivan Show*—and I can tell by your blank expression you have no clue who that was."

Claire laughed. "I've heard the name, that's for sure. But that's as far as it goes."

"Well, back in the day, *The Ed Sullivan Show* was a big deal. The biggest deal, in fact. It was <u>the</u> television show to be on if you were a performer in the '50s and '60s. It could make your career. Or in the case of my pal Jackie Mason, put a serious dent in it."

I smiled at the memory of the late Jackie Mason; Harry had always been fond of the acerbic stand-up comic. The one time I'd met the comedian, he'd been in town for a gig. I'd joined Harry and him at the Lincoln Del restaurant for tons of great pastrami, fascinating road stories and bad jokes.

"Being on *The Ed Sullivan Show* was a huge honor," Harry continued. "The audience was massive—we're talking millions of people tuning in every week—and there were always A-list performers alongside me: Elvis Presley, The Beatles, Bob Hope. My appearance on *The Ed Sullivan Show* certainly helped me take my career to the next level. After that, I went on to perform at some of the most prestigious venues, traveling the world."

"That must have been awesome."

"Well, if by awesome you mean inspiring or impressive—awesome has become a terribly abused word, I'm sad to say—then you are correct.

"I traveled the world with my first wife, Alice, doing shows at some amazing venues. We went to Las Vegas and Atlantic City for casino performances; we did shows in Europe and Asia; we even did a tour through Egypt for two months. It was an incredible experience."

"Wow," Claire said. "That sounds like a dream come true."

"It was," Harry said, his voice filling with pride. "I consider myself very fortunate to have had such an amazing career. And I'm especially proud of the award I received a couple of years ago in London—The Devant Award, named in honor of the first president of the Magic Circle. It's an honor that only a few magicians ever receive, and it is certainly something that will always stay with me."

"Awesome," Claire said and then laughed self-consciously.

"Awesome indeed. I also had the chance a few years earlier to swap magic stories with the then Duke of Cornwall."

"Forgive me," Claire said. "Should I know who that is?"

I could practically hear Harry grinning through the speaker.

"He is more commonly known today as His Royal Majesty, King Charles III."

"Oh. My," Claire said.

"Oh my indeed," Harry echoed.

As we listened to Harry's stories, Nathan and I continued our work cleaning up the shop. We wiped down each shelf meticulously before restocking them with books and magic props and whatever else.

It always surprised me just how much *stuff* was packed into this relatively small space.

However, the Swedish Death Cleanse was proving effective; as we worked through each section of the shop together, the place began to come alive again with color and life—just like Franny had promised it would.

Harry's interview continued as the soundtrack behind our slow and methodical work.

"I know the seniors at Lakeview Haven are always looking for something new to do," Claire said. "Have you ever thought about offering a class on magic?"

The silence with which this question was greeted suggested it had really taken Harry by surprise. Which in itself was no small feat.

"To be honest, Claire, I hadn't ever really considered it."

"Well, I hope you will. I'm sure you've taught before."

"Oh, I have, I have. I've been teaching magic and illusions for years now—I even taught a class at the University of Minnesota back in the day. It was always a great experience; nothing more satisfying than taking someone who has never worked with magic before and showing them how to execute a trick flawlessly. My students were enthusiastic and eager to learn, so it made teaching all the more fun. Of course, that's not to say I was always the most patient of teachers."

Nathan and I exchanged a look.

"That's an understatement," Nathan said with a grin.

Harry paused for a moment before continuing, his voice taking on an almost nostalgic tone. "The best part was seeing my students go on to do amazing things with their magic skills. Many of them have gone on to become professional magicians themselves. And I couldn't be prouder."

Another glance between Nathan and me, this time a silent one. We both knew we wouldn't have any kind of career in magic without Harry. Yes, he was a tough teacher. But there was none better. We nodded to acknowledge this shared thought and returned to our work.

"Well, then, teaching a magic class here at Lakeview Haven could be the perfect opportunity," Claire suggested. "Not only would you be able to share your passion for the craft, but it would provide residents with an enjoyable and stimulating activity. Plus, you never know—you could even inspire someone else to pick up a wand and follow in your footsteps!"

The silence on the Bluetooth speaker suggested Harry was really considering this suggestion.

"You know, Claire, that really is a terrific idea," Harry finally said.

"Well, as the Program Director here at Lakeview Haven, I can get you on the schedule as soon as you've got your class plan ready."

"Oh, it's always ready," Harry chuckled. "I just need to alert my team and we'll be ready to go in the blink of an eye."

Nathan glanced up from behind the counter he was cleaning.

"Harry has a team?" he said, sounding completely puzzled.

I shook my head. "I think he means a team of one," I replied, realizing my fate was already sealed. "I think he means me."

3

"It was like some Jedi mind trick. One minute he's telling me he's going to start teaching a class and the next thing I know I'm recruited as his co-teacher. Which is just Harry's way of calling me his unpaid TA."

I was still trying to wrap my mind around this new development, but Megan seemed more excited than I was.

"What's the class schedule like?" she asked.

"Well, I was thinking it would be like the one he did at the University: that was a three-week class. They'd meet on Monday, Wednesday, and Friday for an hour and a half each time. During the first week, they'd go over the basic principles of magic and illusions. Lots of history. Lots of foundation. The second week, they'd start working on basic moves. Then in the third week, they'd learn a trick."

"But that's not what Harry is planning?"

I shook my head.

"He said we're working on a different time scale with this group. As he put it, 'Most of these folks won't even buy green bananas.' He said they don't have time for history and all that. He wants to jump right into tricks. I'm working on the list of what to bring right now. I just want to make sure I'm not missing anything."

I looked down at the yellow legal pad in front of me, which was going to be my guide as to what items to grab from the store on my way to the first class. It was a pretty thorough and wide-ranging list, offering a broad spectrum of magic effects for the beginning student.

"Harry suggested that I look for tricks that could aid in hand-eye coordination and memory," I said as I glanced up at Megan. "He said the steps had to be simple and easy to recognize, and if performed correctly, they wouldn't fail—at least not catastrophically."

"Qhat have you got so far?"

I read from the list: "A set of Linking Rings. Some rope for The Professor's Nightmare. A deck of cards for an Ambitious Card routine. Some pre-printed grids for calculating and performing The Magic Square. A bucket and some coins for The Miser's Dream. A Zombie Ball. A Square Circle."

I paused, took a breath and continued down the list: "A Multiplying Bottles routine, a few thimbles and a Nest of Boxes, and a wand or two. Oh, and some sponge balls. You can't go far wrong with sponge balls."

I paused and looked up at Megan. "What else should I grab? Or should I just back up a U-Haul truck and bring the whole store?"

Megan smiled and shook her head. "No, that's a great list. The only thing I can think of that might be fun to add is that self-coloring coloring book trick. Their grandkids would love that."

"Brilliant! That should have been the first thing on the list." I added it to the sheet, picked up the pad and headed toward the door.

"I'm going to go to the shop and load up," I said. "I'd offer to pick up anything you might need at the grocery store, but given this list, I doubt there will be room in the car."

* * *

"IT'S NOT A BAD TURNOUT," I said as I scanned the Lakeview Haven Activity Center. At least a half-dozen seniors were milling around the room. A young woman was flitting from senior to senior, jotting the names of each of the attendees down on her clipboard.

I'd been introduced to her when I'd pushed the heavy and wobbly two-wheel cart of magic props into the room. She was the Program Director, Claire, and she was just as upbeat as she'd been on her podcast.

"We're super excited about this," Clair had said immediately. She was in her late twenties, with short brown hair and a bright smile. Her enthusiasm was contagious, even with someone as cynical as me.

I'd helped her and Harry set up a couple rows of chairs and then we moved a table to the front of the room. I assumed this was where he would lecture from.

"So, you're just going to jump right into tricks?" I said to Harry once we'd finished with the room set up. We'd taken two empty chairs off to the side of the room. I was really surprised he was taking this odd approach to the structure of the class. "Usually, you make a student learn at least <u>some</u> history before they can even pick up a deck of cards."

Harry slowly leaned forward in the chair, his face serious.

"In the past," he began, "it was traditional to offer folks who wanted to learn magic a more comprehensive overview of the craft. But this group is different—they aren't magicians-in-training, after all. Just a bunch of grandmas and grandpas wanting to wow their grandchildren with something special.

"So, we need to take great care in what tricks we offer them. For example, Cards Across is a great trick," Harry continued. "But if you really want to learn it, you need multiple performance opportunities. Which means you need multiple audiences. This group simply won't have that. Theirs is a very limited universe.

"But what they do have is plenty of time to practice in private." He paused for moment, thinking. "So, for this class, I want to give them an 'elevated experience' when they perform. Something to really wow their families and friends."

"Something more than The 21 Card Trick," I suggested.

"Exactly."

Claire picked this moment to approach Harry.

"I think they're all here," she said brightly as she double-checked her clipboard. "A couple last questions about the room set-up. If you need it to be darker in here, I can have those blackout shades lowered."

She gestured to the devices at the top of each window in the room.

"We use this room for movie night—which is usually scheduled for Saturday afternoons."

"Movie night is in the afternoon?" I asked.

Claire smiled. "Otherwise, half the audience falls asleep. Anyway, we can make it pretty dark, if you need that."

"Thanks," Harry said as he scanned the room. "But I think the lighting is good as it is."

"Okee-dokee," Claire said. "So that means you probably don't need the projector or the screen?"

He shook his head. "Not today, thanks."

"The sound system? It's Dolby."

"I think we're good."

"Fantastic!" Claire turned and called the group to attention.

"Welcome everyone!" she said, her enthusiasm palpable even several feet away. "Most of you know me: my name is Claire and I'm the Program Director here at Lakeview Haven.

I'm so excited to have you all join us for this special magic class!

"We have two wonderful instructors here today," Claire continued. "This is Harry, the master of the craft who will be teaching us all sorts of tricks with cards and other objects. And this is Eli."

She paused, trying to figure out on the fly what sort of role I was there to play. Nothing must have come to mind, so she simply moved on.

"But before we jump into the magic, why don't each of you tell us your name and why you decided to take this class?"

She gestured to a white-haired gentleman in the front row, who was wearing a bright plaid vest and a brighter red tie.

He slowly got to his feet.

"Hello everyone, I'm Martin. I lost my beloved wife a few months ago and—to be honest—have been feeling quite lonely ever since. My daughter has been pushing me to take some chances and try to get out more. I thought this magic class might be a great place to start meeting new people."

He stood thinking for several more seconds. Then he must have decided that he'd completed his thought and sat down.

"Thank you, Martin," Claire said. "We're so glad you're here." She gestured to a petite woman with silver hair and kind eyes who occupied the other seat in the front row. "How about you, Irma?"

The woman stood up and smiled at the group. "My name is Irma, and I'm taking this class because I've always been fascinated by magic," she said in a soft voice. Everyone in the room leaned forward to hear her better. "Growing up, I used to watch magicians on television with my parents and I would always try to figure out how they did their tricks. Now that I'm retired, I finally have some free time on my hands, so I thought why not take a class? Plus," she said with a twinkle in her eye, "it'll be a great opportunity for me to show off in front of my grandkids."

Claire smiled broadly as Irma re-took her seat. "I think you'll all come away from this experience with some great ways to 'wow' your grandchildren. And, in some cases, great-grand-children."

Claire gestured to the only woman in the second row. She stood up slowly.

"My name is Fatima," she said, her Jamaican accent lilting along with her words. "And I'm here because I want to learn something new. I've been a bank teller for many years, and it's been a fulfilling job. But in my golden years I wanted to challenge myself with something different. I'm excited to see what the class has to offer and if it can bring me some joy in my life."

Fatima smiled at the group before taking her seat again. Claire thanked her warmly and then gestured to a man in the third row.

"Cornelius, how about you?" She turned to Harry and me. "Cornelius is the President of our Resident Board," she offered.

"The Resident President. And the former mayor of Brooklyn Park," Cornelius added as he stood up.

"We all know you were the mayor," Martin said from his seat in the front row. He didn't even turn around as he continued. "You don't have to mention it every time you open your mouth."

"I just wanted to offer a complete and comprehensive CV," Cornelius snapped back. He turned to the rest of the room. "Good morning, everyone," he said in a deep, confident voice. "My name is Cornelius and I'm taking this class because I believe that it can bring me closer to our community. While I'm not a magician myself, I'm hoping this class will give me the skills and knowledge needed to engage with my constituents by performing small tricks at events or gatherings."

He paused for a moment and looked around at the group. "I also hope this class can help open up more conversations between people and reignite an appreciation for the blessings we all have in our lives."

"Blah, blah, blah," Martin mumbled. "Same old same old." He crossed his arms as he slouched back into his chair.

"Thank you, Cornelius. How about you, Dr. Pemberton?" Claire said as she pointed to a man on the aisle.

His was one of the few faces I recognized in the group. He was Harry and Franny's new next-door neighbor. His small dog, Cererbus, lay sleeping quietly at his feet, which was in stark contrast to when I'd first met the dog. At that initial meeting, he did nothing but yip and bark.

"I'm not sure how interested I am in tricks, per se," Dr. Pemberton began. "But to be honest, I have always been drawn to the remarkable history of the magi and their ancestors, the shamanic figures from which they derived. It is my admiration for these ancient cultures—from Egypt to Greece and on to China—that compels me to seek out answers to questions I have pondered for some time: What were these magi capable of? Why did they hold such venerated standing among their people? I'm hoping this class will be my first step in resolving these mysteries."

I leaned over to Harry. "Are you still sure you want to cut the history of magic segment?" I whispered.

In response, he elbowed me in the ribs.

Our murmured exchange appeared to go unnoticed by Claire. She turned to a lone white-haired woman in the fourth row.

"Lisbeth, how about you? Why are you here today?"

The older woman nodded at the group and straightened her back as she slowly stood up. She was wearing a long, navy-blue dress with a white lace collar. Her hair was pulled back in a tight bun, and she wore large, round glasses that made her eyes look like those of an owl.

"I am here because I find new knowledge, no matter what the topic, incredibly invigorating and a great way to stay active and engaged in life. I taught students for over forty years, and it was always such a stimulating experience. Now that I'm in my twilight years, this magic class seemed like the perfect way for me to continue learning something completely new, while also rekindling some of my youthful enthusiasm.

"Plus," she added with a twinkle in her eye, "as others have noted, it's always a treat to be able to 'wow' your grandkids from time to time."

"It is indeed," Claire agreed. She glanced toward the back row of chairs, which held three occupants: Three older, white-haired women, all dressed in variations of black and grey. If I was remembering correctly from the first time I'd seen them—in the garden during our initial tour—they were referred to as The Spring Sisters. Although, one of them had been quick to point out they weren't actual sisters, they appeared to be joined at the hip. And they were ultra-intimidating, both collectively and individually.

As Franny had observed after they'd given their tour of the garden, "Those three have really mastered the art of the spooky vibe."

"April, Mae, June, do you want to tell us why you decided to take this magic class?" Claire asked tentatively.

The three women exchanged a slow look between them, and then the one in the center methodically stood up.

"We're not taking the class," she said. For such a small woman, she possessed a surprisingly loud and raspy voice. "We're just auditing."

"I see," Claire replied. She looked as surprised by their answer as I felt. She turned to Harry. "That's okay, right?"

"Fine by me," Harry said.

"They remind me of the three witches from *MacBeth*," I whispered to Harry.

"Yes, but only if the witches in *MacBeth* were bone-chillingly creepy," he replied quietly.

"Okay then," Claire said, working hard to put a smile back

into her voice. "Let's get started. It's my great pleasure to welcome your instructor, magician Harry Marks."

There was a smattering of applause as Harry slowly stood up.

"Thank you, thank you," Harry said, smiling broadly at the group. "To kick things off, please extend that warm welcome to my nephew, Eli Marks. Eli is going to perform some magic tricks for you, from which you can pick the one trick you'd like to learn."

With that, Harry sat down again, gesturing to me that the stage was all mine.

I immediately understood why Harry had wanted me to be a part of the class: I was here to put on an impromptu magic show for this crowd, employing a variety of props and tricks I hadn't touched in years. If ever.

"Thank you, Harry," I said as I stepped over to the table. "Thank you so very, very much."

If Harry recognized the deep well of sarcasm in my voice, he did a brilliant job of not showing it.

4

"Good morning, everyone," I said, trying to sound more cheerful and upbeat than I felt. "I'm Eli."

"Hello, Eli." This came from Lisbeth in the fourth row. If I was remembering correctly, she was the former teacher.

Great. A former teacher. I was teaching in front of a teacher. Yet another unneeded layer of pressure. Thanks, Harry.

"What I thought I would do today is run through a few standard magic tricks, to see which ones—if any—capture your fancy. Then we can drill down on the ones you like and figure out which trick you want to hone and perfect. How does that sound?"

This produced murmurs of agreement from the small crowd. Claire, who had stationed herself by the door, gave me a big smile and a thumbs up.

"Well, let's just start with ..." I turned and looked at the array of tricks I had brought over from the store. Had I known I was going to be performing each and every blessed one of them, I might have been more discriminating in my selection process. But, as the saying goes, that was then and this is now.

I was tempted to just close my eyes and grab one at random,

but realized immediately that approach would only hurt one person: me.

So instead, like a mindless bird, I simply reached for the shiniest object.

"Let's start with a classic: The Linking Rings."

I picked up the set of five steel rings and—working hard to drag the routine from my oh-so fuzzy memory—I started to walk through the trick.

When I was younger, I was fortunate enough to witness Jay Marshall perform his awe-inspiring rendition of The Linking Rings. His skill in manipulating the rings with such fluidity and grace—and unexpected humor—was remarkable, and the audience was spellbound by his performance.

I would be the first to admit that what I did paled in comparison, and I can't see anyone disagreeing with that self-assessment. My audience wasn't spellbound, but at least they stayed awake. My version got the job done and produced some polite applause at the end.

And so it went as I performed abbreviated versions of every trick I'd brought along.

I executed a pretty sloppy Zombie Ball routine ... fumbled my way through the brand-new Square Circle illusion I'd just purchased (after recently smashing to pieces the old one I'd been trying to sell for years) ... and then inadvertently revealed the secret of the Self-Coloring Coloring Book while trying to perform it.

As a sort of mental sorbet (and, frankly, out of sheer desperation) I did my version of The Miser's Dream, a routine I performed often enough to consider it a part of my standard repertoire.

And for just a few moments I felt on solid ground.

I used Martin in the front row as my subject and produced coins out of the air—and from the folds of his brightly-colored vest—before dropping them with a solid 'clink' into the metal bucket.

This produced 'oohs' and 'aahs' from the small group and a continuous stream of giggles from Fatima in the second row. She was the one who said she'd been a bank teller for years and she seemed to get the greatest pleasure watching me pull coins out of thin air.

For a few moments at least, I felt like a half-way decent performer.

And then it was onto a botched version of the Multiplying Bottles routine which I concluded with the always inspiring, "Well, you get the idea."

As badly as I felt about my performance, you wouldn't have known it from the audience response. Even something as basic as sponge balls—which I did with Cornelius as my volunteer—produced laughter and applause. Or disgust, in the case of the leering Spring Sisters in the back row. None of the three women had cracked anything resembling a smile as I'd gamely soldiered through all the props.

In contrast, Cornelius hooted with laughter when a small explosion of red sponge balls erupted from his hand as he unclenched his fist. Even his obvious nemesis, Martin, couldn't help but laugh at the large man's reaction to the standard trick.

I was reminded, yet again, that even something as basic as Sponge Balls—which is usually relegated to the world of children's magic and sneered at by <u>real</u> magicians—can blow the socks off a regular audience member.

I glanced over at Harry and his look said it all: You always learn as much or more than the students when you teach magic.

Feeling like I was starting to get on a roll, I pulled out the three ropes needed for The Professor's Nightmare routine. I had performed this trick since my teens and—even though I hadn't done it in a while—my muscle memory pulled me through it.

It's a great trick and a real audience favorite. The premise is simplicity itself: Three different length ropes transform back and forth into the same size ... then into a single rope ... and then back to their original sizes.

Like The Miser's Dream, it was one of the few tricks I demonstrated for this small group where it felt like I was giving an actual performance.

Martin, in the front row, even blurted out "Ooh, I like that one," at the conclusion of the routine, which produced a laugh from the crowd.

Like any performer who wants to end on a big finish, I segued right into my Invisible Deck routine. And like any not-too-bright performer who wants to win the whole audience over, I picked the most finicky attendees as my quote-unquote 'volunteers.'

Why I picked the Spring Sisters I'll never really understand. Maybe it was an intense need to be loved by every member of the audience. Maybe it was some form of self-flagellation.

Regardless of why I did it, it was a bad idea.

There are a lot of variations on the Invisible Deck routine. I have a couple versions that I do, one which is very long and involved. And one that is short and to the point.

I opted for the shorter version because it works well with more than one volunteer.

I approached the three women, having no idea which one was April, which one was Mae or which one was June. A better magician would have asked their names and committed them to memory for the duration of the routine. Of course, a better magician would also have picked more willing and enthusiastic volunteers.

Since I was apparently unwilling to ask their names, in my

mind they simply became the one on the left, the one on the right and the one in the middle.

The three Spring Sisters each possessed the exact same aura of intimidation and judgement. I could almost feel it in the air as they sat there, eyes focused on me like lasers. I took a deep breath.

"So, let's do a little experiment in imagination," I began, instantly regretting my choice of words. I have come to loathe magicians who begin routines with "let's try a little experiment." It seemed like lazy writing.

But, in for a penny, in for a pound.

"Let's try a little experiment in imagination," I repeated. "First, I want you to imagine that I'm holding an invisible deck of cards in my hand."

I held out my empty palm and looked down at it, knowing that most audiences will always look where the magician is looking.

Not these ladies. I glanced up and they were still staring daggers at me. It may have been my imagination, but I was beginning to feel actual heat on my face; it was if their staring powers included some sort of supernatural component. Or I might simply have been nervous and a little flushed.

I did my best to ignore it and pressed on.

I asked the one on the right to think of the suit of a card that might be found in the invisible deck in my hand.

She stared at me for a long moment, and I began to think she might not have heard me. Or was simply unwilling to play along. And then, suddenly, she spoke.

"Diamonds," she blurted out, somehow making it sound like a threat. She glared at the other two to see if either one was going to challenge her selection.

I suddenly got the sense they might be as intimidated by each other as we were of them.

She received no objection from her comrades and turned

back to me. "Diamonds," she repeated, this time even more defiantly.

"Diamonds it is," I said. I turned to the woman on the left. "Now I need you to think of a value for the card. Ace through king. What do you think it should be—?"

"Queen," she snapped before I had even finished my instructions. She didn't bother looking at the other two for agreement. This was a woman who knew her mind.

"Okay, so we've got the Queen of Diamonds," I said. I looked at the woman in the middle, who met my gaze with a steely scrutiny of her own.

"I want you to picture that card—the Queen of Diamonds—in your mind. Really visualize it. Can you see it."

"If I must."

"Terrific," I said. "Now imagine that you're flipping the card over and slipping it somewhere in this invisible deck of cards I hold in my hand. Have you done that?"

She shook her head in disgust. "Yes. Done."

"Terrific," I repeated. I needed to come up with another positive sounding rejoinder, but the vibe coming off the Spring Sisters wasn't helping.

"Now here's where imagination meets reality." I did a sloppy pass over my palm, revealing that it now held an actual deck of cards. This produced a nice "ooh" from the other seniors in the room. But nothing from the Spring Sisters. Which shouldn't have surprised me.

I quickly opened the box and pulled out the deck. As I did, I looked at the woman on the right.

"You picked Diamonds, correct?"

She simply stared back it me. I kept going, trying to give the impression that I wasn't requiring an answer, just confirming a selection. I turned to the one on the left.

"And you picked the Queen, am I right? Of course I am," I said, barreling ahead. I looked at the old woman in the middle.

"And in your mind, you took that card and flipped it over in the invisible deck. How amazed would you be to find that not only is there one card reversed in this deck ..."

I spread the cards face up, revealing that one card indeed was facing the other direction.

"... but that the card is, in fact, the Queen of Diamonds. How amazed would you be?"

I flipped that card over, revealing it to be the predicted card: The Queen of Diamonds.

"Pretty amazing, am I right?"

The three women just stared back at me.

The one in the middle finally spoke. "We're just auditing."

Harry chose this moment to finally come to my rescue.

"Thank you, Eli. Let's take a short break and then each of you gets to pick the trick you want to work on."

While the seniors filed across the room to feast on weak lemonade and stale cookies, I collapsed into the nearest chair.

A few moments later, Harry settled into the seat next to me.

"Been in the war, have we?"

"I know there's no such thing as Magic Boot Camp, but I feel like I just did thirteen weeks of basic training."

"And you lived to tell the tale. Well, to continue your military analogy, 'At ease, soldier.' I'll take over from here."

* * *

TRUE TO HIS WORD, Harry ran the rest of the class meeting, while I slumped in the corner, metaphorically licking my figurative wounds.

"Thank you, Eli, for taking us through all those magical options," Harry said as he began the second half of the class. "Let's give him a well-deserved round of applause."

Harry led the small group, who all seemed to be clapping with actual enthusiasm. Claire, of course, clapped louder and longer than the rest. If I had to predict, I would guess she had been a cheerleader in high school. She had clearly found her calling here at Lakeview Haven.

I nodded and smiled weakly.

"Now comes the difficult part," Harry continued. "I need each of you to pick which specific trick you'd like to learn from the rich cornucopia Eli presented. And remember, just because someone else picks it doesn't mean that trick is off the table for you. If all the magicians in the world had to do tricks which no one else was performing ... well, there would be a whole lot fewer magicians in the world, I can say that for sure. Maybe only one or two."

Harry turned and winked at me, and then directed his attention to the white-haired man in the front row.

"I don't want to put you on the spot, Martin, but someone has to go first. Did any of the tricks you just saw speak to you?"

This was greeted with a longer pause than I'd anticipated. I could feel the tension in the room as everyone waited for Martin to announce his choice. He nervously shifted his weight from side to side in his chair and, for the first time, I noticed his hands were shaking slightly.

He cleared his throat before he began speaking.

"It's just that...I don't think I have the skill to do any of these tricks," he said quietly. He looked away from Harry, not wanting to make eye contact. His voice was filled with defeat and disappointment; it seemed like he had already given up without even giving it a try.

"Oh, now, now," Harry said reassuringly. "None of us thought we could do the tricks when we started, right Eli?"

He glanced at me for confirmation, and I gave him an enthusiastic nod. "That's right."

Harry turned back to Martin. "It's just a magic trick, Martin. Even children can do magic tricks."

Martin's voice came out as a loud whisper. "I liked the one with the ropes," he finally said.

"The Professor's Nightmare," Harry offered as he made a note on a small pad he was carrying. "A good choice. A classic. I believe you will, as the saying goes, kill it." He turned to Irma.

"And for you?"

She didn't have to think about it at all. "The one with the coloring book," she said quickly.

"The Self-Coloring Coloring Book. Excellent selection."

"I think my grandkids will get a kick out of it," Irma said.

"I think they will indeed," Harry agreed. He looked to Fatima in the second row. "Now, Fatima, I don't want to influence your decision in any way, but if I had to make a prediction, I would say you're going to choose The Miser's Dream. Am I right?"

"Is that the one with the coins?" she said, unable to hold back a giggle. "Yes, if it's the one with the coins." She continued to chuckle at the memory of the routine.

"The Miser's Dream is indeed the one with the coins," Harry agreed as he made a note on his pad.

"Can I do the one with the sponges?"

This came from Lisbeth, the former teacher. She seemed nervous that her request might be denied.

But of course, it wasn't.

"By all means, Lisbeth. Sponge balls it is," Harry declared as he made a note on his pad. He turned to Cornelius. "And for you, sir?"

"Well, there were many wonderful options, to be sure," Cornelius began. "And I'd like to think I could master any one of them. And perhaps I will; a late-in-life shift to magic might be just the thing. But I think the one that spoke to me the most was the Linking Rings. There is something so graceful and elegant about it."

He paused for a moment before continuing. "It's hard to

explain exactly why that trick speaks to me as it does, but I think it has something to do with my desire to connect with people on a more meaningful level. The Linking Rings are a physical representation of that connection—if you will—and I want to use them as a way of expressing, in a physical form, that connection with people that I am always seeking."

"Oh, blow it out your constituency," Martin grumbled from the front row.

Harry, wisely, ignored that remark.

"The Linking Rings," he said as he noted it on his pad. "A good, if challenging, choice."

"I'm up to the challenge," Cornelius said proudly.

"I do not doubt that, I do not doubt that for one second," Harry said as he moved across the room. "Now, Dr. Pemberton, what trick have you selected?"

Pemberton looked up at Harry and shook his head. "I don't want to be a troublemaker, but I was hoping there would be a trick where I could use these. Something where I could really focus on them."

From where I sat, he appeared to have a few large coins in his hand. Harry picked one up and examined it.

"A Kennedy half dollar," Harry said as he flipped the coin over.

"I have four of them," Pemberton explained. "My late wife, she got them from her father. They sat on her dresser for years and years. I'd like to do something with them, but not that Miser Dream thing. There's too many coins in that one."

"Yes, that's clearly the point in The Miser's Dream. A cascade of coins," Harry said as he continued to gaze at the half dollar. I could tell he was running scenarios through his mind.

"I don't mean to be a troublemaker."

Harry smiled at Pemberton. "You're not a troublemaker, Dr. Pemberton. You are a man who wants to honor his late wife's memory. And I am sure we can find something that will do just that. In fact, I believe I know the perfect trick for you."

He turned to me. "What would you say, Eli?"

"Well, it's a little advanced for a beginner, but my first thought was Sympathetic Coins."

"And that was my first thought as well," Harry agreed. He turned back to Dr. Pemberton. "Yank Hoe's Sympathetic Coins trick is perfect for you. We will go into more detail on that tomorrow."

He made another note on his pad and then turned to the Spring Sisters.

"You're just auditing, correct?"

The three scary women nodded in unison.

"Excellent," Harry said as he quickly reviewed his notes. "For our next step, we'll be doing one-on-one sessions with each of you tomorrow, to go into greater depth on the tricks you've selected. See Claire on your way out to set up your specific time slot. Eli, do you have anything else to add."

I was surprised by the question, but not by my answer. I was exhausted.

"I do not."

"Excellent. Class dismissed."

5

I swung by the magic shop first thing the next morning, to drop off all the extra tricks and props which were no longer needed for Harry's magic class at Lakeview Haven.

I discovered Nathan was already there, futzing with some boxes piled up on the main display counter.

"Good morning," I said as I glanced around the shop. "Wow, the shop looks great. You got a lot of cleaning done yesterday while I was gone."

"Didn't clean. I spent the day going over the new tricks that showed up."

"Really?"

"Yep." Nathan looked up at me, with one raised eyebrow. "You thought I spent the day cleaning. And wanted to encourage me to keep at it while you're gone today. Right?"

"You caught me."

"Nice try. I spent my day reviewing tricks."

Nathan was well into his first year of writing trick reviews for *Genii* magazine. Although he was a man of few words in conversation, Nathan really came to life in print, generating reviews of several hundred words, offering his thoughts on the pros and cons on new magic tricks which were just hitting the market.

"Anything fun come in?"

Nathan shrugged. "A bunch of new coin gimmicks, nothing too earth-shattering. A new self-solving Rubik's cube."

"As if we needed another one."

"Yep," he agreed. "Oh, this one was kind of fun, in a geeky sort of way. Grab that deck of cards and come down to this end of the counter."

I picked up the box of cards he'd indicated and followed him down the counter to a clear space.

He took the deck of cards, slid the cards out and riffled them in front of me, face up.

"Go ahead, just pick one of the cards as I flip through them."

I knew what he was doing and how he was doing it, but I played along and pretended to be a layperson.

"Did you spot one you liked?" he asked once he'd finished riffling through the deck.

"I did."

"Don't tell me what it is. Just think about it. Really concentrate on it."

Although I'd given that same instructions hundreds—maybe thousands—of times, I couldn't help mentally going through the motions. I thought about the card I'd seen.

"You've heard about the mind-body connection, right?" he asked.

I nodded.

"Well, there's a theory that sometimes your mind can manifest something on your body, if you think about it hard enough," Nathan continued. "Like, remember when the words "Help Me" appeared on the little girl's stomach in *The Exorcist*?"

I nodded. I was intrigued; I couldn't see where this was headed. And when it comes to card tricks, that rarely happens anymore. I am usually several miles ahead of the performer, waiting patiently for them to catch up.

"Are you thinking about the card you spotted?"

I nodded. I was. I was thinking about the Three of Spades. And I knew that Nathan knew I was thinking about the Three of Spades.

"Well, let's see if your body is manifesting what your mind is thinking."

Nathan pulled out his phone and clicked an icon on the screen. The flashlight popped on, although I immediately recognized that the light coming out looked a little different.

"This is a UV light, which will react to heat changes on your body," he said as he scanned the light up one of my arms and then down the other. He focused it for a moment on the back of my right hand.

"There's something going on here," he said slowly. "Can you flip your hand over?"

I did as instructed, opening the palm of my hand to his light.

I blinked.

There, in the center of my hand, was a "3" and the symbol of a spade. It was sketchy, but it was clearly there. Under the light, it glowed bright blue. And then, as he turned the light away, it completely disappeared.

"Okay, I'm impressed," I said as I held up my hand. Nothing was visible on my palm. I turned it this way and that, but the image didn't reappear.

"Simplicity itself," Nathan said as he clicked off the light on his phone. "A phosphorus stamp on the top of the card box puts the image of the Three of Spades on the palm of your hand when you pick up the deck. And an app converts your phone's flashlight into a UV light."

"Impressive."

Nathan shrugged. "I think it has its uses. The only downside

I've noticed so far is that it's a bear to get it off your hand. I've washed my hands several times—and showered—since I tried it out yesterday, and it's still not quite gone."

To prove his point, he flipped the flashlight on again and directed it toward the palm of his hand. Although it wasn't as prominent as it had been on my hand, the image of the "3" and the spade was still noticeable.

"So, I'm going to ding the product on that," he continued. "But other than that, it's clever and it's at a nice price point."

"And it doesn't feel too techie," I added.

"That's right. Not like this new book test," he said, pointing to his iPad further along the counter. "You let the volunteer flip through your eBook collection on your tablet or phone. They pick any book. They pick any page. They pick any word on that page. And you're able to predict exactly what word they picked."

"Oh, that's too techie," I agreed. "Or, as Harry would say, it's too perfect."

"Too perfect indeed. But look at this." Nathan moved down a few steps to show me one more item: It was a shopping bag made of a thick paper stock, which lay flat on the counter.

He held up the bag, spun it around so that I could see all sides, and then he shook it open. He looked up toward the ceiling and his eyes appeared to be tracking a falling object. The bag jumped a bit in his hands, as if something heavy had just been tossed into it.

He reached into the bag.

And pulled out a cantaloupe.

He handed it to me.

It was, in fact, a real cantaloupe.

"Sweet," I said as I hefted the melon. "Although, to be fair, you could make one of those bags yourself. The info and the specs are out there."

"Agreed. But this is a great product if you're not into arts and crafts. And it's at a nice price point."

"So, you're going to spend the day writing reviews?"

"That's the plan. You?"

"One-on-one magic lessons with Harry and the students from his Lakeview Haven magic class."

"If you're both going to be there, isn't it really two-on-one?"

I shrugged. "I hope so. I was cast adrift yesterday and was pretty much on my own."

Nathan grinned. "Not to worry. When it comes to the nuts and bolts of teaching magic, Harry is incapable of remaining silent."

* * *

NATHAN WAS RIGHT.

While the previous day's class had been essentially the Eli Show, Harry immediately took the lead with the one-on-one lessons.

When I arrived at the Activities Room, Harry was in conversation with Claire.

"Good morning, Eli!" Harry said brightly. "We're just going over the schedule for the day's sessions."

"I hope to hang out for most of the morning, if that's okay," Claire said. "This is really fascinating."

"You are most welcome, dear."

"I'll have to sneak out to help deliver some breakfasts and I think I'm helping in the dining room at lunch. But if you stick to the schedule, you'll probably be having lunch at that point anyway."

"Oh, I suspect we'll stay right on schedule." Harry said. And then he suddenly went a little pale. "By the pricking of my thumbs, something fearsome this way comes," he mumbled quietly.

I turned to see The Spring Sisters had entered the room. Their arrival surprised us all; so much so that Claire actually consulted her list to see if they were in fact part of the schedule.

"Good morning, ladies," Claire said tentatively. "Are you looking for an activity this morning?"

"We're here for the magic class," the one in the middle said, her voice a smoky rasp.

"Well, Mr. Marks is doing one-on-one lessons today, so there isn't a group meeting."

"We thought we'd audit the one-on-ones," she replied flatly. Not a question, simply a statement of fact.

Claire looked over at Harry, a look of confusion across her face. "What do you think, Harry?"

"The more the merrier, I suppose," Harry said, somehow putting an ironic spin on the word 'merrier.'

The Spring Sisters took their traditional seats in the back just as our first student—Irma—showed up. Given her age, I was surprised at the speed with which she entered the room.

"Good morning, Irma," Harry said, grinning broadly. "Ready to learn the secrets of the Self-Coloring Coloring Book?"

I winced, but only a bit. I had pretty much given away the secrets of the Coloring Book illusion during my lame presentation the day before. Either Harry didn't remember my gaffe or he was thoughtfully ignoring it.

"I can hardly wait," Irma said, a nervous tremor in her voice. "I raced through breakfast to get here, that's how excited I am!"

"Well, then, let's get cracking," Harry said as he clapped his hands together. "Eli, be a good fellow and grab the coloring book, will you?"

And we were off and running.

It was a revelation.

I had never seen this side of Harry before. Instead of his usual gruff exterior, he was warm and delightful—nothing like the Harry I had grown up with.

The truth was, I had learned nearly everything I knew about magic from Harry. And it had not always been a joyful experience. Aunt Alice had always said that—when it came to teaching magic—Harry lacked the three Ps: Patience, Praise and Positive Reinforcement.

However, he now somehow had all those qualities in abundance here in the Lakeview Haven Activities Room.

He was a picture of patience with Irma as he walked her first through the mechanics of the coloring book, and then offered suggestions on the performance of the piece.

"The key is to make every move look natural. You move the position of your hands on an off-beat, or gesture with the hand and then return it to its next location."

Under his guidance, Irma picked up the nuances quickly. And throughout, Harry was patient, offering frequent praise and then reinforcing that praise again and again.

This new Harry was also there for Fatima, who struggled at first with the mechanics of The Miser's Dream. This was due—in no small part—to the fact that the trick required first learning how to produce a coin from thin air ... and <u>then</u> learning how to make it seem like you were actually depositing it into the bucket.

Fatima was a slow learner. And throughout it all, Harry was the picture of patience.

"You are really getting it, Fatima," Harry said as the end of the session approached.

"I don't believe that is as near the truth as you suggest," she said. It was clear she was struggling.

"Let me ask you this," Harry said softly. "When you first became a teller at the bank, how quickly could you make change?"

"Oh, my," she said with a laugh. "I was so slow. So, so slow. It was painful to watch me, I'm sure."

"But I'm guessing you got better at it and eventually muscle memory took over, am I right? And after that point, you didn't even have to think about it while you did it."

Fatima nodded. "That is true. It became second nature."

"Well, the same can be true of The Miser's Dream," Harry said as he patted her hand. And then he gave her the same advice he would give every student that day: "Work on it on your own tonight and tomorrow. And I think you'll be surprised how much you've improved when we reconvene on Thursday as a group."

As Fatima left the Activities Room, she had already started practicing: As she headed down the hall, I could see her working on plucking a coin out of thin air. And even though it had been a tough lesson, she was still giggling as she went.

Next up was Lisbeth, the former teacher who had opted to learn a sponge ball routine.

She was right on time and started talking as soon as she came in.

"I can't lie. I may have cheated a bit," she said.

"And how would one do that?" Harry asked smiling. "I believe you wanted to work with sponge balls, right?"

"I did. I do. But I went ahead and looked at some videos on the YouTube."

It was all I could do to suppress an audible gasp. Experience had taught me Harry was no fan of learning magic from the Internet; not because he was against video training, but because of who was doing it."

"With all due respect," he said once when the subject had come up. "But why would anyone want to learn a trick from someone who, in all likelihood, only learned it himself within the last hour or so? And learned it incorrectly to boot?"

However, although I anticipated an explosion after hearing Lisbeth's confession, no such eruption was forthcoming. Harry only grinned and led her toward the table.

"Not a problem at all," he said. "You were a teacher and I

think you might agree with me on this: It is sometimes easier to teach someone who has already started learning a subject as opposed to someone who is a complete blank slate."

It took a moment for this concept to settle in, but when it did, Lisbeth began to nod and laugh.

"You know, Harry, I think you're absolutely right on that."

Harry laughed with the older woman. And then they got down to the specifics of the lesson, giggling and having a great time throughout.

Like I said, the Harry Marks I was witnessing in the Activity Room was not a Harry Marks I had ever experienced in the past.

6

Somehow the one-on-one sessions appeared to have been scheduled along gender lines.

After we'd finished seeing the three older women, the first of the three men showed up: Martin, who walked so slowly down the hall toward us, I was afraid his session would be over before he made it to the door.

Claire had been in and out of the room all morning ("I should have asked more closely what 'Other Duties As Assigned' meant on my job description," she'd said with a laugh the first time she'd had to leave). But by the time the men started showing up, she had become a fixture, sitting quietly off to one side.

The presence of the Spring Sisters was just as persistent, but far less reassuring. They sat in the back, the picture of creepy stillness, like a stone sentinel silently judging as the morning progressed.

Claire jumped up and met Martin halfway down the hall, chatting with him amiably as she guided him toward the room. Once inside, she brought him over to the table in the center of the room where the lessons were taking place.

"The Professor's Nightmare was your choice, if I'm not mistaken," Harry said once Martin was seated.

"Yes," Martin said. "I was surprised Professor Pemberton didn't latch onto that one, but I suppose that might have been a bit too on-the nose."

"Perhaps," Harry agreed with a smile.

While the two older men chatted, I grabbed the three lengths of rope necessary to perform The Professor's Nightmare and placed them in front of Harry on the table.

"Well, let's get to it, shall we?" Harry said as he picked up the ropes.

"I am in your hands," Martin said, trying to work up a smile. "But, as I mentioned, I don't really have a great deal of faith in my abilities in this one area."

"Well, who knows. You may surprise yourself."

And with that, the lesson began.

Martin might have been a bit slow on his feet, but his mind was as sharp as ever. Harry walked him through the routine and Martin quickly picked up on the steps—even adding in some of his own touches along the way.

Despite the passing of years, he clearly still possessed the agility to do the trick with little effort. In a matter of minutes, he had sufficiently mastered all the key steps in the effect.

"Well, this is certainly easier than I expected," Martin said after a successful attempt at one of the key moves.

"It helps that you are a bit of a natural," Harry said.

Martin's eyes widened in surprise. "You really think so?"

"I'm sure of it," Harry replied confidently. He glanced my way. "Don't you agree, Eli?"

"Absolutely," I said from the far end of the table. "He has a real knack for this."

"Well, you know," Martin said as he began to run through the routine again. "Once you learn the secret, it's really a bit disappointing. I expected something more ... I don't know ... magical."

"And therein, Martin, lies the greatest lesson in magic you may ever learn," Harry said. "And it's one you need to make your peace with early on. It is this: The secret to the illusion is rarely as magical as we've led the audience to believe. You mustn't let your understanding of just how—to be blunt —stupid the mechanics are have any impact on the quality of your performance. The moment you do, you're dead in the water as a performer.

"As they old saying goes," Harry continued, "a magician is merely an actor pretending to be a magician."

* * *

MARTIN HAD BEEN a quick study when it came to learning how to perform The Professor's Nightmare with skill and panache.

Our next senior student, Cornelius, was the flip side of that coin.

The former mayor of Brooklyn Park's journey toward learning his trick was one of trials and tribulations, with more lows than highs.

I quickly realized—and I'm certain Harry recognized it as well—that Cornelius was the worst kind of terrible performer: The type who imagines himself a superstar.

His choice of The Linking Rings may have been part of the problem, but I'm honestly not sure any other trick could have played to his limited strengths.

For all his bombast—and don't kid yourself, the former Mayor of Brooklyn Park had plenty of bombast—he was simply a klutz, with no real connection between his mind and his hands.

Harry was the picture of patience as he walked the large man through the steps of a very simple, three-ring Linking

Rings routine. Harry explained the concept of the key ring, the handling of the rings, and the moves necessary to create the impression of penetration and separation.

Harry might as well have been talking to a wall.

Cornelius was so convinced of his natural talents that I'm not sure he heard half of what Harry had to say. And the half he did hear, he misconstrued.

All the while, The Spring Sisters sat in silent judgement. I had to admit, if they were the first audience I'd ever performed magic in front of, I might have done as badly as Cornelius did with The Linking Rings.

Have I spent a more painful hour? Perhaps. I once had a molar removed under what I'm convinced was some sort of numbing placebo. But watching Harry try to teach Cornelius this simple routine came in a close second.

The only thing that made it any easier to bear was the man's blissful ignorance as to how badly he was doing.

Instead, at times it felt like he was the one trying to teach Harry. He would finish my uncle's sentences, ignore his suggestions, and just blindly bang the poor rings together like a mechanical monkey beating on a drum.

And all the while, he grinned from ear to ear. He thought he was fantastic.

The lesson came to a merciful conclusion with the arrival of Dr. Pemberton.

"Well, it looks like our next student has arrived," Harry said quickly as soon as he spotted the white-haired man in the doorway. "You just keep doing what you're doing, and we'll see how it all looks on Thursday."

"Thursday, Smursday," Cornelius said with a laugh. "If you ask me, I'm ready for the Vegas stage right now."

"Indeed. That will be our loss," was all Harry said in response.

And then we were onto our final student of the day.

* * *

"I HOPE I'm not creating extra work for you," Dr. Pemberton said as he sat across the table from Harry. "I mean, wanting to learn something using my wife's coins."

"Oh, perish the thought," Harry replied as he settled back into his own seat. "The greatest gift an educator can give is connecting the student with their passion."

"I could not agree more," Pemberton replied with a wide smile. "Harry, I believe you and I are cut from the same cloth." He glanced in my direction. "And this beamish boy doesn't fall far from the tree."

"I'll accept the beamish, but challenge you on the boy," Harry replied.

"Does anyone need any coffee or water or anything?" Claire asked as she re-entered the room. She'd responded to a text on her phone during the debacle with Cornelius and had been spared much of that tortuous session.

Or ... she had merely pretended to get a text, and wisely escaped when she could. An excuse I wished I'd had the good sense to fabricate.

Regardless, she was back now.

We all thanked her for the offer of a beverage—including the Spring Sisters, who scowled in response to her suggestion, which she took to mean 'no.'

"I called a dear friend of mine last night," Harry began. "A brilliant coin performer named Sam Esbjornson. And he suggested a version of The Sympathetic Coins which I think would nicely fit your beginner's status."

"I'm all ears," Pemberton said as he pulled out his four half-dollars. "And, of course, I've brought my coins." He glanced over at Claire. "Claire, have you ever seen a US half-dollar? Or are those currencies completely outside of your daily commerce?"

He held the coins up as she stepped closer to the table.

"You know, I've heard of them, but I don't think I've actually ever seen or used one."

"These are John F. Kennedy half-dollars, minted circa 1964," Pemberton said as he handed her the four coins. "Unfortunately, that denomination fell out of favor in the 1990s. By 2002, I believe they had stopped making them altogether."

"Are they worth something?" Claire asked as she flipped one of the coins over. "My dad was big into coin collecting."

"Oh, I imagine they would fetch anywhere from fifty cents to twenty dollars, depending on the condition," Pemberton explained. "For me, their value is entirely sentimental."

"Which makes them quite valuable indeed," Harry said. "Now, Dr. Pemberton, I must commend you. Inadvertently or not, you just executed a flawless convincer for this trick. Before it's even commenced, no less."

Pemberton raised an eyebrow as Clair handed back the coins. "A convincer? Which is what, pray tell?"

"A convincer answers an audience question before they're even aware they want to ask it," Harry explained. "In this instance, by talking about the history of the Kennedy half-dollar—and letting the coins be casually and closely examined —you've convinced the audience that you aren't working with gaffed—that is, tricked—coins. Before they have even considered that notion, you've already convinced them otherwise."

"Well, bully for me," Pemberton said with a grin. "Aren't I the smart one."

"With that key lesson learned, let's dive into the basics of what will become your version of The Sympathetic Coins."

Harry grabbed the coins and then performed a flawless rendition of the trick.

He spread a dark, square handkerchief on the table between himself and Pemberton, as Claire observed from over the professor's shoulder.

Harry then placed one coin near each of the cloth's four

corners, leaving enough room so that he could turn back each corner so that it covered its respective coin. Once all four coins were covered, he waved his hand over three of the corners, miming the invisible transfer of each coin to the fourth corner.

He then pulled back those corners, revealing that those three coins were, in fact, gone.

With a flourish, Harry pulled back the remaining corner of the handkerchief. All four half-dollars were revealed to have assembled under the fabric.

This produced a yelp and spontaneous applause from Claire. For his part, Pemberton let out a smile as he shook his head in disbelief.

"You possess some mysterious sorcery, sir," he whispered, his eyes widening in awe. "Witchery, I say. Pure witchery."

"Sorry, it's nothing quite so exotic, I'm afraid," Harry said as he moved the coins back to the center of the cloth. "A little sleight of hand, a sprinkle of misdirection and the deed is done. Let me take you through the steps and you'll see what I mean."

With that, Harry went through a complete tutorial on the trick, explaining each move thoroughly as Dr. Pemberton looked on. He was the only student so far who had felt it necessary to take notes; he scribbled little feathery scratchings in a small, worn leather notebook, glancing up as Harry offered suggestions to make all the moves appear more natural.

Back and forth they went, with Harry demonstrating and Pemberton copying each move, repeating it again and again.

Before the prescribed hour was done, the old professor was able to perform a passable version of the routine; although there was the slightest tremble in his hands, it appeared to have no impact on his performance abilities.

"That's all for today," Harry said after a near perfect performance on his student's part. "I want you to practice it tonight and tomorrow. We'll reconvene on Thursday as a group, for performances and assessments."

"I look forward to it," Pemberton said as he scooped up the four coins. "It will be fascinating to see how each of us has progressed on our chosen illusion."

"Indeed, it will," Harry agreed as he accompanied Pemberton toward the door.

As with all of Harry's plans, this one felt particularly right, especially for these students: teach them the basics of a trick ... and then provide ample time for them to get the moves engrained into their muscle memory.

There was only one flaw in his plan.

As it turned out, not all of Harry's students would be around for the next class session.

7

The bulk of Wednesday was spent with Nathan, continuing our Swedish Death Cleanse of the magic shop.

On the plus side, progress was made.

On the downside, by the end of the day we'd only gotten through about half of the store.

As we worked, I kept a written inventory of larger issues which needed addressing.

The carpet had to go. It had been there since I was a teenager and it had literally worn out its welcome.

The displays in the front windows needed a massive over-haul. The arrangement of the tricks and props was haphazard at best, and many of them had been deeply faded by years of persistent glare from the sun. And some were older than me and in worse shape.

The items on the Gags & Gifts shelf needed to be brought into the current century. Many were no longer funny, if they ever really had been. And although one or two had literally saved my life, I wondered on a more global scale if these types of products were really representative of what I wanted the magic store to be?

Nathan leaned over and glanced at my list.

"You realize that for every task we've accomplish, your list adds two more?"

"I'm beginning to recognize that. What's the solution?"

"Simple. Stop making lists."

I couldn't find any holes in his reasoning.

I folded the sheet of paper in half and then half again, stuck it in my pocket and continued with the legion of cleaning tasks which lay before me.

* * *

THE NEXT DAY, when I got to the Activities Room at Lakeview Haven, Harry was already there, as was Lisbeth. He was demonstrating a finer point of the sponge ball routine for her.

She nodded along enthusiastically as she watched his hands closely. "Oh, I see where I went astray," she said. "I need to already have the sponge ball in place at that point."

"Indeed," Harry said. "It's called the One Ahead principle. I may spend a couple minutes on that concept this morning, as it applies to more than just the routine you're working on."

"What's that, you're going to discuss magic theory?" I said in mock surprise. "What was it you said about not buying green bananas?"

"I'm just offering a sprinkling of context, not a master's course," Harry said quietly.

I had no snappy comeback, which was just as well, as Cornelius chose that moment to enter. He clanged his three large metal rings loudly as he crossed the room.

"Learn a magic trick? Mission accomplished," he said loudly. "I am ready to demonstrate my prowess to all and sundry."

"And we can't wait to see what you've come up with," Harry said with a grin. I doubt Cornelius recognized the sarcasm in Harry's tone, but I heard it loud and clear.

Cornelius was followed by Dr. Pemberton, who strolled in alongside Fatima.

"You have done wonderful work on your trick," she said to the older man. She swung her metal bucket as she walked; I could hear the coins clinking around within. "It's funny that we both chose tricks with coins, but I don't think they could be more different."

"I've been thinking along those exact lines," Pemberton said. "How each of us picked the illusion which somehow reflects an aspect of our personality. An intriguing notion ..."

He paused and gave a thoughtful smile, then continued. "You, after years in banking, literally making money appear at your fingertips. Cornelius and The Linking Rings—an outwardly simple display which represents seamlessly joining people and policies. Lisbeth and her sponge balls—the former teacher, making ideas magically multiply in her hands. And me, with my silly coins ..."

He opened his hand which held his four half-dollars. "Well, I'm not entirely certain what my trick represents."

"Sorry I'm late," Irma said, pushing past Pemberton as she made her way into the room. She held the over-sized Coloring Book in her hands. "I had them bring breakfast to my room this morning and they were running late for some reason."

"Not to worry, we're not all here yet," Harry said as he held out a chair for her. "Take a seat."

He looked to the others and gestured they should all sit down.

"I'm so curious to hear how your practicing went yesterday," Harry continued as he rested on the edge of the table.

"Fantastic," Cornelius said immediately. "Couldn't have gone better."

"It was a long day for me," Fatima countered. "Slow going. By the evening, I think I was seeing some progress, but it was a long day."

"There will be fewer and fewer of those, trust me," Harry said quietly.

"I was surprised how much standing in front of the mirror helped," Irma offered. "You were right."

"Videotaping yourself is also a terrific tool," Harry said. "We can get into more detail on that later. Dr. Pemberton?"

"Well, I worked on it on my own in the morning," he began slowly. "And then I transgressed a bit."

"Oh? How so?"

"You had instructed us to simply practice the routine on our own," Pemberton said. "Which I did for a while. A good long while, to be sure. But it was driving me to distraction. So— forgive me father, for I have sinned—I went to the dining room and tried it on a couple people there."

This revelation produced an audible response from the rest of the small assembly—a group gasp. Harry grinned and shook his head.

"And I learned so much, almost immediately," Pemberton continued quickly. "It is an entirely different experience with an audience watching your every blessed move."

"Burning you?" Harry suggested.

"Exactly, well put," Pemberton agreed. "Their beady little eyes burning right through your hands as you try to make the moves. But I persevered. And the dining room was a terrific location, with residents coming and going. And the poor kitchen staff—I must have done the trick for everyone on duty yesterday, from Chef to dishwasher. But it didn't stop there!"

"Do tell," Harry said. I sensed he was enjoying Pemberton's confession.

"Oh, I performed it for the concierge staff, from Big Steve right through the entire front office. For a passing tour group.

For the folks in maintenance. I even cornered poor Ruby and made her—and her entire cleaning crew—endure the bloody thing. By the time I got to Mikos, the gardener, I realized I had literally run out of audiences."

"And what was the upshot of all that transgression?" Harry probed as he leaned forward a bit.

Pemberton considered this. "I got better," he finally said. "But not just better. My performance improved exponentially. By a factor of ten at least."

"There endeth the lesson," Harry said as he sat back and scanned the small group. "I am a true believer in practice and rehearsal, but there is nothing—nothing—that will make you a better magician faster than putting yourself in front of the unwashed masses. So, as you perform what you've learned in front of your peers this morning, think of this as your first public performance." Harry glanced at Dr. Pemberton. "Well, the first public performance for most of you."

This produced a laugh from the group; Dr. Pemberton hung his head in mock shame but joined in the laughter as well.

The echo of that laughter was still resonating when Claire entered the room.

She stood in the doorway for a long moment. Her expression told me immediately that something was wrong.

Harry was the next one to notice her, and his mood shifted immediately when he saw the look on her face.

Slowly, the rest of the class turned as the laughter died down. Cornelius, still grinning, was the last to look toward the doorway.

"What is it, Claire?" Harry asked.

"This morning, when they went to bring Martin his breakfast, he didn't answer. So, the staff member used their pass key and entered his apartment."

If was clear she was having trouble with this announcement.

As she spoke, the Spring Sisters appeared behind her in the hallway, approaching like ghostly phantoms. They stopped in their tracks, sensing something of import was being discussed.

Claire was finally able to find the words. "I'm sorry to say, but at some point during the night, Martin passed away."

8

Claire's announcement ended the magic class for that day.

Clearly no one was in the mood, and it just didn't seem appropriate.

"We'll reconvene on Monday morning," Harry announced quietly as the class members began to file out of the room.

Claire and I watched them go, and then I approached Harry.

"Do you think I should call Deirdre? To speed things up?" I turned to Clair to explain. "My ex-wife is an Assistant District Attorney, and her current husband works in Homicide."

Claire nodded at me blankly.

Harry gently put his hand on my back. "I don't think that will be required in this instance, Eli."

"But Martin is dead. They'll want to investigate, won't they?"

Harry smiled at me wryly. "Eli, when was the last time you were involved in a death which was clearly the result of natural causes?"

I had to think about that for a long moment. It had certainly been a while. Quite a while, in fact.

"That would be Max," I finally concluded. "When your friend Max died."

"Well, natural death may be a rare occurrence for you, but it's a matter of routine around here. Isn't that so, Claire?"

She nodded. "Sadly, yes."

"The fact is, not all deaths are crime scenes. Most of them, in fact, are not."

"Maybe that's why they call them natural?" I suggested.

"Yes, exactly." Harry turned to Claire. "Now, about juggling the class timetable ..."

While Harry and Claire quietly conferred on the implications of this sudden change in scheduling, I considered Harry's comment.

It really had been quite a while since I'd experienced a death of the natural variety. And I wasn't sure I actually remembered how to deal with it.

Well, I thought, I guess this would be my chance.

It was what my Aunt Alice would have called a learning opportunity.

"Claire says there will be a short remembrance this afternoon in the chapel," Harry said after the young woman left. "I plan to attend; I hope you can come as well."

"No problem. That's a pretty quick turnaround for a service."

"Claire said it's the custom around here. A few of the residents may go offsite when the funeral comes around, but most would rather remember their friend right away, here at home. A charming custom, really.

"Besides, it should be interesting," Harry continued. "The last time either one of us were in a chapel, was when we married our respective brides in the Wedding Chapel at The Mall of America."

"Because Franny had a coupon," I added.

Harry smiled at the memory. "And who says frugality and

romance don't mix?"

* * *

THE CHAPEL at Lakeview Haven was nothing like the one at The Mall of America, in all the best ways.

The stain glass windows were genuine, the music came courtesy of a live organist, and there were no screaming teenagers on amusement park rides thirty feet away to interfere with the service.

On the whole, it was a decidedly informal affair, with people gathering and chatting warmly before the short program.

It was odd, I thought, to be at an event like this when all the mourners were just that: mourners. They weren't also suspects, as had so often been the case in the past.

It was a whole new way of looking at the world.

All the surviving members of the magic class were in attendance; even the auditing Spring Sisters put in an appearance, cloaked in their usual dark attire, silently evaluating the proceedings.

Claire was there, of course. She seemed to be in charge of moving things along. The sales agent who'd given us the original tour of the place, Samantha, was there as well, flitting from small group to small group. Always selling, always closing.

I recognized a couple people from the Concierge staff—including Big Steve—and Ruby, an imposing woman who was in charge of the cleaning crew. She and Franny had bonded over the use of organic cleaning fluids early after Franny's arrival at Lakeview Haven, and I think they were on their way to becoming friends.

Many of the kitchen staff were also in attendance, along with Chef Anton. Their presence seemed to be focused on preparing and replenishing an impressive display of snacks in the back of the chapel. This area of the room was clearly the most popular and for many appeared to be the highlight of the event.

I stood with Harry and Franny in a far corner, observing the interactions throughout the room. Although a somber mood pervaded the gathering, there was also more than a smattering of laughter here and there.

"I suspect this won't be the first one these we'll be attending," Franny said quietly.

"I suspect you are correct," Harry replied. "It comes with the territory. Put a couple hundred old people in one place, you're going to have an occasional memorial service."

"It's not a memorial service," said a nearby voice. We turned to see Dr. Pemberton strolling by, drink in hand. He stopped and leaned into our small group. "That term is verboten around here."

"Oh, that's right," Harry said quickly. "Claire mentioned that. They call it a Celebration of Life, not a memorial service."

"Why in heavens name is that?" Franny asked.

"For the self-same reason they'd prefer we don't mention heaven," Pemberton said with a wry smile. "Here at Lakeview, they take the concept of nondenominational to the nth degree. Just uttering the word 'memorial,' for some reason, makes certain people uncomfortable. Even though it is not, per se, a religious term. It comes from the Latin—*memorialis*, which means 'of or belonging to memory.'

"The party line seems to be that it's safer to ignore all faiths in lieu of inadvertently favoring any one of them," Pemberton continued. "I'm still surprised the stained glass made it past the Nonsectarian Chapel Committee. I believed the only reason these windows survived was due to the high cost of replacing them. As determined by an emergency meeting of the Building Beautification Committee."

"The Nonsectarian Chapel Committee? The Building Beautification Committee?" I repeated.

"Eli, understand this: the fine folks here at Lakeview have taken committee creation to the level of an art," Pemberton said with a smile. "There is—and I kid you not—even a Committee on Committees, which oversees the legion of delegations which are the lifeblood of this fine establishment."

Before I could delve further into this with Dr. Pemberton, Claire began the program.

She welcomed the attendees and asked us to take our seats. People obediently began to slide into the hard, wooden pews. I found a spot for Franny and Harry, while Dr. Pemberton indicated he preferred to stand.

The format appeared to be one of quiet reflection (with soothing but nonreligious organ music as the soundtrack), peppered with occasional remarks from the assembled crowd about the deceased.

Every few minutes, another elderly person would wander to the lectern and recount a memory of Martin (and his late wife) from their time at Lakeview Haven. And then a few more quiet moments, with just the organ music.

It felt like the whole thing was about to conclude when I noticed Dr. Pemberton headed toward the front of the room. He still had his drink in his hand.

"One final thought, if I may," he said as he scanned the group. "We have spent much of this afternoon talking about Martin's days here at Lakeview Haven. However, this was only a brief moment in the story of the man's life. It was just one bend on the river of his existence. Before this point, there were raging rapids and tranquil eddies; bright sunshine and deep shadows. Those of us who had the pleasure of knowing him—however briefly—got a small sense of all that had come before. It is often said that we should not dwell in the past, yet I believe our past shapes who we are. Therefore, we should embrace it and share it whenever possible."

He took a long sip of his drink and then held his glass up in a toast.

"In the words of Lewis Carroll: "It's no use going back to yesterday, because I was a different person then.""

With that, Pemberton gave the slightest of bows and stepped away from the lectern.

"Thank you, Dr. Pemberton," Claire said as she returned to the front of the room. "And thanks to all of you for sharing your thoughts on Martin. This concludes the formal portion of our program. There are refreshments in the back of the room. Thank you for coming."

* * *

WHILE OTHERS LINGERED to finish the delicious snacks crafted by the kitchen staff, I followed Franny, Harry, and Dr. Pemberton as we sauntered through the garden and back towards the main building.

Franny and Harry seemed to have taken a strong liking to their new neighbor. His refined speech and formal mannerisms would have been intimidating in the classroom, but—as someone who had never sought a significant college-GPA—I found his presence delightful.

"You know, it was around this time a mere nine months ago that Martin and I partook in two similar gatherings; first for Martin's wife, Irene. And too soon thereafter, for my Bernice. I wouldn't say Martin and I were ever close, but that one-two punch certainly pulled us a little tighter."

"I can see how that would," Harry said quietly.

"Mikos, you never fail to surprise and delight," Franny said loudly and suddenly. "The garden looks like Eden itself."

The tanned, older gardener was coming toward us, a coil of wire fencing in one hand. He smiled at the compliment.

"Thank you. It is always one thing or it is another thing," he said in his thick Greek accent as he trudged past us. "Today, my nemesis are the rabbits. They have taken a sudden, persistent interest in my beloved, my lovely ladies, making much of one plant disappear. Why have they picked now to ravage my beloved, I don't know. They never touched it before. But this, I think, will prevent any further damage."

He gestured to the wire fencing in his hand as he veered off the path toward the section which included the purple, bell-shaped flowers he had pointed out to us on our first tour.

"Best of luck with that," Franny offered as we continued on our way.

"I imagine you dealt with rabbits on a daily basis in your trade," Pemberton said to Harry. "Pulling them out of hats and so forth?"

"That's a trick performed more in legend than in reality," Harry offered. "Although, we did for a time have a rabbit as part of our children's show. Until I got tired of him upstaging me."

"Harvey," I said, thinking back on the rabbit. He had retired from the act about the same time I'd moved in with Uncle Harry and Aunt Alice.

"Never perform with children or animals is the old saw," Harry continued. "My variation on that is that one should never perform <u>with</u> animals <u>for</u> children. Nothing will sidetrack your show faster."

"Noted," Pemberton said with a chuckle. "Eli, I hope you can join us for dinner."

I glanced at my watch. I knew two things for sure: Megan was working late at her store. And we had nothing but leftover pizza in the fridge.

"I'd love to, if you'll have me."

"The more the merrier," Pemberton said. "Of course, today <u>merrier</u> is a relative term."

* * *

"WHY IS it that a celebration of life only makes me think about death?" This question came from Dr. Pemberton after another long sip of port.

"I believe that is what they call an unintended consequence," Harry replied.

After a truly sumptuous dinner, Harry, Dr. Pemberton and I had retired to the Library. Franny begged off, citing the need for her presence at that evening's meeting of the Holidays (Except Christmas) Committee, of which she had somehow become the Chair. Tonight's key agenda item was the need to upgrade the Halloween decorations.

As the sun set, the library transformed into a different world. The large windows no longer allowed in any light, so only small table lamps positioned throughout the room provided illumination. This created mysterious shadows in between the rows of bookshelves and dark wood furniture. The crackling of logs in the fireplace was the only sound punctuating our conversation.

Dr. Pemberton had brought a bottle of port along for our post-dinner conversation, and between the three of us we'd already made a good dent in its contents.

I was a novice when it came to port; I'd seen it in old films, but this was my first time tasting it. When I inquired what port was exactly, Dr. Pemberton offered an extensive answer without hesitation.

"Port is a wine which has undergone a vinification process that involves fortifying with brandy," he explained. "This supplementation of the alcohol content inhibits the fermentation and preserves the natural sugars in the grapes, thus contributing to the port's distinctive taste profile."

I nodded, not at all sure what he'd just said.

"Well, it's nice," was all I could come up with. Harry grinned at me.

During dinner, Dr. Pemberton had done plenty of this sort

of speechifying. And the more wine he drank, the more elaborate his monologues became.

This included an intense conversation with Chef Anton—who delivered our meals to our table personally—about the relative merits of cilantro ("Highly overrated," according to Pemberton) which the Chef endured with an affable grin.

"You know when I lost my faith in humanity?" Pemberton said moments after finishing his dissertation on the origins of port. "I can pinpoint the moment: It was when people stopped using turn signals."

"You can pinpoint it to that moment, can you?" Harry said. I could tell he was enjoying winding the other fellow up a bit.

"I can," Pemberton said. He had placed his half-dollars on the small table next to his chair and took this moment to pick one up for closer examination. Harry mirrored the action, taking one coin to look at as well.

"It seems to me that often the most straightforward act of kindness to your fellow human being is somehow the hardest," Pemberton said. "Using your turn signal is a prime example. Its steady use could, unquestionably, make the world run smoother. Yet still a significant percentage of people on this planet are unwilling to do it. To me, this suggests that we—as a society—have missed some fundamental lessons along the way and are heading towards an inevitable decline. If we haven't arrived there already."

"On the other hand," Harry said as he flipped the coin over. "These coins are filthy. When was the last time you cleaned them?"

Harry has always been something of a fanatic about working with clean coins. And well-ironed silks. And a million other nitpicky details of magic performance. I was somehow pleased to see that even his new, senior citizen students weren't going to be spared this side of him.

"A year from never would be my guess," Pemberton offered.

"Ironically, these coins have been in more hands over the last two days than in the last fifty years, I'm sure of that."

"What do you say I polish them up for you?" Harry suggested. "I have all the tools."

"That would be a kindness," Pemberton said as he slid the rest of the coins across the table toward Harry.

"And speaking of coins," Harry said. "That friend I mentioned, the one who suggested the version of The Sympathetic Coins I taught you—"

"For which I am eternally grateful," Pemberton interjected.

"No problem," Harry continued. "But Sam—Sam Esbjornson—has volunteered to swing by and give you some one-on-one tips on coin handling. If you want. He's willing to do the same with Fatima and her Miser's Dream routine."

"Wow," I said quietly.

Pemberton looked over at me, one eyebrow arched. "This Sam Esbjornson is of such a caliber that his very name inspires an exhortation as profound as ... *wow*?"

"He is indeed," I said. "I once called him the David Roth of the Midwest, but he quickly corrected me. 'Not on your life. I prefer to think of Roth as the Esbjornson of the East Coast.'"

Harry smiled. "I imagine there is no art or craft or endeavor which doesn't inspire some level of internal professional jealously."

"Academia being the worst," Pemberton said as he took another sip. And then he let out a long sigh. "What a day. You know, in this life, we are utterly ill-prepared for aging and dying. And when you think about it, it's really the only thing we should be preparing for."

"Here, here," Harry agreed as he raised his glass.

Mine was empty, so I reached for the bottle Pemberton had brought. I splashed the equivalent of a few more sips of the dark liquid into the glass.

"When I think of all the books and papers I've written on

various facets of philosophy over the years, there really is only one I should have attempted: a guide to aging and dying," Pemberton said. His face lit up for a moment. "I even have a terrific title."

"Lay it on us," Harry said.

"It's going to be called *This is My First Time Getting Old (so excuse me if I go astray).*"

"That's a million-seller title," Harry said. "I'd buy two."

"I've learned so much," Pemberton continued quietly as he took another sip. "And all too late."

A few minutes later, with the bottle of port well drained, we headed back to the residential wing of the building. Our first order of business was to pour Dr. Pemberton back into his apartment, to make sure he got in safely.

He fumbled a bit with the lock but eventually he got the door open. We were greeted by Cerberus, who gave the three of us the once over and decided that—since we were a known quantity—barking was not required.

Once we got Dr. Pemberton into his apartment, we moved to the next door. Harry had no trouble with the key or the lock.

"Eli, I think you need to spend the night in the spare room."

"I don't want to put you out."

"The reason we got the two-bedroom apartment was for nights like this. I won't take no for an answer."

And I was in no shape to argue.

I placed a quick call to Megan to let her in on the plan. And ten minutes later I was in the spare bed and drifting toward what felt like a deep and deathlike sleep.

That was when the sound from next door jolted me straight up in bed.

It was Pemberton.

And he was screaming.

9

Harry and I met each other in the hallway outside the bedrooms; he was in his bathrobe, while I was in a t-shirt and boxer shorts.

"I think it came from next door, Dr. Pemberton's apartment," Harry said breathlessly as we headed toward the front door.

Once in the main hallway, Harry banged on his neighbor's door. "Charles, it's Harry. Are you all right in there?"

There may have been the sound of a distant whimper, but I wasn't really sure. Harry gave the door handle a fruitless turn. Then he looked at me.

"I think he sometimes keeps the French doors to the garden ajar. In case Cerberus needs to go out."

"Good thought," I said as I raced back to Harry's apartment. Through the living room. Out the French doors.

The wet grass squished around my bare toes as I sprinted to the next set of doors. Harry had been right: the doors were ajar.

I pushed my way into Dr. Pemberton's dark apartment.

"Dr. Pemberton?" I said loudly as I fumbled and stumbled my way through the living room.

"He was here!" came a weak cry from a distant room. "Right here!"

I followed the sound as best I could, realizing quickly that Pemberton's apartment was the mirror image of Harry and Franny's place. What would have been a left turn to get to their bedrooms was a right turn here. Feeling my way through the living room, I stubbed a bare toe on a table leg and let out a yelp.

I heard panting at my feet, which told me Cerberus was in the room. I followed his outline in the dim moonlight and soon I was in front of the bedroom door.

I pushed the door open.

Dr. Pemberton was huddled in the corner of the bedroom, his hair disheveled and eyes wide with terror. He was wearing pajamas, and the bedsheets were jumbled up near where he had been sitting—a telltale sign of someone who had recently and hastily jumped out of bed.

"Dr. Pemberton, are you okay?" I asked, trying to keep my voice soothing.

"He was here," Pemberton said, his voice quaking. "Right here in the room with me."

I scanned the area again, still not spotting anything unusual. My eyes had grown somewhat adjusted to the dim lighting. I could tell that, apart from the tiny dog, we were the only ones in the room.

"Who was here?" I asked as I moved toward the quivering old man crouched near the floor.

"It was Death," he rasped. "Death was here."

* * *

By the time I was able to get Dr. Pemberton off the floor and onto the edge of the bed, Harry had arrived.

"How's he doing?" he asked.

"He's in a state of shock," I said, looking over at Harry. "He keeps saying Death was here."

Harry's face grew serious. "What do you mean? Like, the Grim Reaper?"

Dr. Pemberton nodded frantically, his eyes wide and terrified. "He was here in my room, standing over me. I could feel his cold breath on my face." His head jerked from side to side as he quickly scanned the dark, empty room.

Harry and I exchanged a glance.

"Did you see anything else?" I asked, hoping for more useful information.

Dr. Pemberton shook his head. "No, just Death. He was here to take me away. Last night he came for Martin. His apartment is directly overhead. Tonight, he came for me. Maybe last night was a mistake. Maybe last night was supposed to be me and not Martin. I don't know what to do."

Harry and I exchanged another look. This was getting odder by the second.

"Listen, Charles," Harry said, his voice gentle but firm. "We're going to stay with you tonight. We won't let anything happen to you. I promise."

Dr. Pemberton's eyes darted between us, as if weighing his options. Finally, he nodded slowly. "Okay. Thank you."

With a little coaxing, I was able to persuade the trembling man to get back into bed and under the covers. Despite the obvious rush of adrenaline racing through his system, he slipped into a fitful sleep faster than I had anticipated.

Once we were sure he had successfully drifted off to sleep, Harry and I moved to the living room to confer.

"Was it the port? It seemed to me he had been drinking most of the afternoon and into the evening. Maybe the port pushed him over the edge?"

"Maybe," Harry said. "But I've dealt with plenty of drunks over the years, many far more sloshed than the good doctor in there. This was more than a drunken dream. I would say it bordered on a hallucination of some kind."

"That might suggest some sort of neurological issue, right?"

"Possibly. It certainly suggests the need for a full check-up at the very least. Unless ..." He scratched at his beard as he tipped his head back in thought. "Occam's razor."

"The idea that the simplest explanation is usually the correct one?"

"Yes. In this case, I think it would be prudent to consider if there may be an alternate explanation for what happened here tonight."

"Like, was there actually someone in the room?" I suggested. "An actual person? A burglar or something? And Pemberton simply misconstrued what he was seeing?"

"Possibly," Harry said. "Although, while both of us heard Pemberton scream, I don't think either of us heard Cerberus bark."

"Which he would have done if someone had broken in."

"Which brings us back to the idea of a possible hallucination," Harry said. "But if it was a hallucination, what triggered it? It can't just be the port. There has to be something more."

Harry sighed slowly as he surveyed his surroundings. Everything in the apartment was arranged neatly, from the furniture to the wall decorations. Pemberton had a thing for pop art, with one of Roy Lichtenstein's comic book prints covering most of one wall, and three smaller prints on the opposite side.

"However, I think we've done all we can do for tonight. In the meantime, let's keep an eye on Pemberton. Make sure he's okay."

We both headed back to the bedroom to check on the doctor.

As we entered the room, it was clear that while he may have fallen asleep, this was not a peaceful slumber. Dr. Pemberton had tossed and turned so much that the bedsheets had become twisted around him. He was murmuring to himself, his eyes fluttering behind closed lids.

I moved closer, trying to catch what he was saying. It was difficult to make out at first, but then I heard it.

"Death comes like the thief in the night," he whispered hoarsely. "He comes for us all in the end."

I exchanged a worried look with Harry. Pemberton was clearly still deeply disturbed by whatever had happened.

"Hey, Charles," Harry said softly as he approached the bed. "It's okay. You're safe here with us."

But Dr. Pemberton didn't seem to hear him. He continued to murmur to himself, his eyes still closed.

"Death comes for us all," he repeated. "He comes for us all."

As we turned to leave, I couldn't shake the feeling of unease that had settled in my gut.

Something was definitely not right here.

10

"You look like a terrific candidate for some coffee this morning."

I looked up to see the Sales Manager—Samantha—standing next to my table. She had a coffee pot in her hand and a too-bright smile on her face.

"That is exactly what I need," I said as I flipped the cup over in its saucer and pushed it in her direction. "You're on dining room duty today?"

"We all work everywhere around here. Pitch in when needed."

"'Other tasks as assigned?'"

"Precisely," she said as she expertly filled the cup. "They've even got Big Steve working the breakfast buffet this morning."

She tilted her head in that direction, and I turned to see the small man was indeed serving eggs, sausage and other offerings to a short line of residents. His head was barely visible above the serving station.

"Give me a wave when you need a refill." Samantha said as she headed toward the next table.

My reply was drowned out by the coffee as I took the first few life-restoring sips.

"If you ask me, that doesn't sound like the result of alcohol," Franny said as she and Harry took their seats at the table. They each carried plates ladened with food from the breakfast buffet. Franny looked over at me. "Aren't you eating, Eli?"

I shook my head and immediately thought better of it. "Not just yet."

"You know the expression 'Any port in a storm?' Well, I think it was the port itself that did Eli in last night," Harry said with a chuckle.

"Too bad. You're missing some great food. It's one of their theme days. Big Steve is serving a genuine English breakfast. The real thing: fried eggs, bacon, sausages, black pudding, mushrooms, baked beans and toast. It's enough to make your mouth water just by looking at it!"

Franny held the plate under my nose and I instinctively pulled back. It was bad enough to have a hangover; adding a traditional English breakfast was just this side of cruel.

"So, you don't think what Pemberton experienced last night was alcohol related?" Harry said as he popped a cooked mushroom into his mouth.

"It doesn't sound like it," Franny said. "It really sounds like a drug-induced hallucination. I mean, I don't think the alcohol helped."

"It certainly didn't help me," I said as I took another long sip of coffee.

"Top of the morning to all," came a booming voice behind me. It was so loud and so sudden it nearly shook the coffee cup right out of my hands.

Cornelius slid into the seat next to me.

"What a magical table this is," he said, then slapped my back as he burst out laughing.

First the English Breakfast and now someone laughing

loudly, slapping me, and shouting in my ear. I had to get out of here.

I took the last sip of my coffee. "I think I better head over to the shop."

"You do that, and I'm going to head over and grab some grub," Cornelius said with another unnecessary laugh. He placed a meaty hand on my shoulder and used what was left of my body to push himself to his feet.

Moments later he was gone, although his voice was still making my ears ring. I turned to Harry.

"Call me later and let me know how Dr. Pemberton is doing," I said as I started to stand.

"Stick around. You can ask him yourself."

I turned and saw Pemberton making his way towards us. As per usual, he was wearing a suit, looking as though he was about to give a classroom lecture instead of taking part in the morning meal at this senior living community. Still, something wasn't quite right with him. His hair had been hastily combed and there was stubble on his face which suggested he'd forgotten to shave. His eyes were bleary and bloodshot and looked unfocused.

"Good morning, all," he said quietly. "I see we all survived the night."

"We did indeed, although I had my concerns about you," Harry said. "How are you doing?"

Pemberton shook his head slowly as he steadied himself on the chair next to me.

"Upright and taking food," he said. "At least, I'll attempt food. I have only sketchy memories of what happened last night—what was real and what was part of a twisted dream-scape—but I remember two things for sure: The terrifying figure of Death. And that you both were there. And for that I thank you."

"How much do you remember?"

"I remember being terrified by the vision—or the reality—of Death, standing at the end of my bed," he began. "It felt very real. Terrifyingly real. Then I remember waking up screaming. And I remember you both helping me get back to sleep. The rest is silence.

"You can fill me in on any of the other gory details which may have escaped me," he continued. "But first, I am in need of sustenance. Or, at the very least, what passes for sustenance here at Lakeview."

Pemberton cautiously ambled towards the food selection, steadying himself with a chair here and there along the way. As he departed, Harry turned his attention back to us.

"It was drugs," Franny said quietly.

"Perhaps. Or perhaps it's something deeper," Harry said quietly.

"Maybe it's something medical," I offered. "Something treatable."

Harry nodded as he considered this.

"Let's hope that's it."

* * *

SOMETHING WAS DIFFERENT. That registered immediately.

Had I been a bit more on the ball, I might have noticed the changes to the display in the front windows earlier. But, as my head was still as scrambled as the eggs I had avoided for breakfast, it wasn't until I had my hand on the front door handle of Chicago Magic that I realized things were not the same as I had left them.

I stepped back several feet, so I could see both window displays—on either side of the door—at the same time. If I had taken one step further back, I might have tumbled backward off the curb. But I didn't notice. Or care. I was entirely transfixed by what I was seeing.

The displays had been completely revamped.

Gone were the old, dust-covered gags and knickknacks. The sagging stuffed rabbit in the top hat was no more. And the faded shelf paper that used to line the bottom of each display had been swapped out for a polished silver material that glinted in the sunlight.

Behind everything hung beautiful velvet curtains in deep shades of blue and red which seemed to shimmer with their own light. The whole scene was a sparkling, magical wonderland that made my heart beat faster.

The mundane cardboard "Open" sign in the window had been changed to a bright neon 3D one, emitting a shining glow that enticed people to come inside. It was a welcoming sign, inviting customers in before they even crossed the threshold of the store.

I stepped through the door and was surprised that the interior of the shop also looked brighter. A quick glance around revealed that everything was still the same as yesterday; the only difference was that Nathan had replaced most of the dusty fluorescent bulbs. He was atop a ladder, inserting the final bulb when I came in.

"The windows look amazing," I said, not even trying to hide the excitement in my voice. "I thought we might do a little cleaning, a little dusting, get rid of some of the faded props. But you've completely reimagined them. They're gorgeous."

"Thanks," was his single-word reply. But I could tell he was pleased at my reaction.

"I thought you had a lot of writing to do yesterday," I continued. "How did you find time to completely re-do the window displays and also write those *Genii* reviews?"

Nathan slowly and carefully stepped down each rung of the ladder.

"I discovered something about myself yesterday: You know what I like to do more than writing?"

"What?"

"Anything!" he declared, getting about as loud as Nathan ever gets. "I like to do <u>anything</u> if it means I have an excuse not to write. And yesterday, that anything was re-doing the front window displays."

"I have that same relationship, in magic, when it comes to practicing. Harry once said that he thought I brought procrastination to a high art."

"Well, that was how I spent my day. So now I'm a day behind on the reviews, but at least the window displays are done."

"And all the lightbulbs are cleaned and/or replaced."

"Exactly."

There were a few moments of silence as we each scanned the shop.

"Why don't we do this," I finally offered. "You have a better idea of what still needs to be cleaned here in the shop than I do. Why don't you just act as Project Manager today and be the one to assign me tasks. And then, that will free you up to write, but also give you that much-needed occasional distraction from writing."

"I like the sound of that," Nathan said.

"Where should I start?"

Nathan turned and looked at a yellow legal pad on the counter.

"You're gonna hate it."

"I'm sure I will, but whatever it is, it has to be done."

"Okay," he said with a long sigh. "You know the back room?"

"I do indeed. I've been here since I was thirteen."

"Well, that was probably the last time a key part of the backroom has been cleaned."

It took a moment and then I knew what he meant.

"The bathroom."

"Yes, the bathroom back there needs to be cleaned. It resembles a Turkish prison. And it's the next thing on the list."

To prove to me he wasn't lying, he held up the yellow pad and pointed to the first item which hadn't been crossed out.

Harry used to say that he'd installed that bathroom to save his marriage.

Back when he was hosting magic meetings nearly every week, along with offering one-on-one lessons, he'd send magicians in need of a bathroom up the long flight of stairs to the apartment he shared with Aunt Alice.

She put up with this steady stream of socially challenged young men for about two weeks, and then issued an ultimatum: Either the meetings moved to another location, or Harry had to install a bathroom in the backroom.

"You know, it might be easier to just get some bricks and seal it up like they did with Tutankhamen's tomb," I offered.

"Do whatever you need to do so we can cross it off this list," was Nathan's response. "Now I've got to get those reviews written."

* * *

I WAS able to take a break from the Swedish Death Cleanse the next day, because I'd offered to chauffeur Sam Esbjornson over to Lakeview Haven. He had agreed to do one-on-one coin sessions with both Fatima and Dr. Pemberton.

I had known Sam since I was a teenager, and most of what I knew about coin magic was due to his teachings. Much like my uncle Harry, Sam was what the two of them called 'magic famous.' With audiences made up of non-magicians, Sam would be treated with the same respect you'd show any elderly gentleman. However, when put in a room with a group of magicians, it was as if Mick Jagger had just walked in—Sam's fame was palpable.

He managed his celebrity status with modesty, becoming renowned for his generosity in sharing knowledge with any magician—professional or novice alike—on how to better their coin magic craft.

But in my world, he was also renowned for his insistence on being the lead navigator whenever he was in a car. He may not have been the driver, but he wanted to be in charge of how we got to wherever we were going. If he had a theme song, it would have been "My Way."

His biggest bugaboo was left turns. Sam would go miles out of his way to avoid having to make a left turn. He argued that it had been established—through scientific testing—that avoiding left turns would reduce your risk of being injured in a crash.

I'd never been in an accident while Sam was navigating, so it was a tough point to argue.

From the moment he got in the car that morning, he had a detailed plan on how to get to Lakeview Haven while making the least number of left turns possible.

I'd realized years ago it was best to not argue and instead just do as he said. So, despite arriving a bit late, we got there without any disagreements (and precious few left turns), which I thought was a reasonable compromise.

"Pretty swanky," Sam said as we made our way from the visitor's parking lot. "Is everyone settling in?"

"I think Franny is loving it," I said. "For Harry, the jury's still out."

"Well, you'll have to give me the full tour, if there's time," Sam said. "I might be ready to sell the house and downsize my life."

"I know Harry would love that," I said. "If he could get all the Minneapolis Mystics to move in here, he'd be thrilled."

As we made our way past the garden toward the main entrance, I saw Mikos slowly moving across the lawn. As before, he was carrying small segments of thin wiring fencing. He noticed us and gave me a wave.

"The rabbits, they persist, I don't know why," he said as he gestured toward the fencing he'd already constructed around one patch of flowers. "They vex me, but I will win. I will protect my lovely ladies. This I promise you."

When we got to the Activities Room, I was surprised to see that Franny was there, along with Harry and Dr. Pemberton. And then I nearly did a double take when Pemberton looked up from his seat at the table.

If he had been a little disheveled the previous morning, he was now a complete mess. His clothes were wrinkled, and his hair was standing up in all directions. He had dark circles under his eyes, and it looked like he had been up all night. He gave me the slightest of smiles.

"What's going on?" I asked as we crossed the room.

"I had another visit last night, just like the night before. Death came into my room, and he was looking for something."

"What was he looking for?" I asked.

Pemberton didn't just look unnerved. He looked absolutely terrified.

"I think he was looking for me."

11

"It was a long night," Harry said as he patted Pemberton lightly on the back.

"And there was no alcohol," Franny added. "We were with him until ten, when we called it a night."

"And then at midnight he awoke us with his screams," Harry said.

"I'm so sorry," Pemberton said. "I have no idea what's going on."

"Well, first thing Monday morning, you're headed to the doctor for a full workup," Franny said.

"If I make it to Monday," Pemberton said with a dark chuckle.

"Keep talking like that and we're headed to the ER right now," Franny shot back.

"Thank you, thank you both so much," Pemberton said quietly. He turned toward Sam and me. "And you must be the legendary Sam Esbjornson."

"Legendary in my mind, at least," Sam said.

"Thank you so much for offering to spend some time with

me," Pemberton said as he shook Sam's hand. "The Sympathetic Coins routine has been the one bright spot this week."

"Well, it's a lovely routine. Should we jump right in?" Sam suggested with a glance toward Harry.

"No time like the present," Harry said.

Sam sat at the table, directly across from Pemberton. "To start off, why don't you just show me how you're currently performing the routine?"

"It's been a couple days, so I suspect I'll be a bit rusty," Pemberton began, and then he looked toward Harry. "Did you bring the coins?"

"I did indeed," Harry said as he reached into his pants pocket. He pulled out the four coins and handed them to Dr. Pemberton as he looked over at Sam. "I gave the coins a good cleaning and a polish. I know how you abhor a dirty coin."

"A dirty coin is the worst. You can't do strong magic with dirty coins."

"These look lovely, Harry, thank you so much," Pemberton said as he looked over the coins. He held them out to Sam. "The first thing I do is I hand out the coins for examination by an audience member. I ask them if they are familiar with the Kennedy half-dollar. And then I might give a little history on the coin."

"Excellent notion," Sam said as he examined the coins. "Always a good idea to slip those convincers in early."

"Well, apparently I stumbled into that," Pemberton said, smiling for the first time since I'd come in. "Purely accidental, but Harry was quick to point out the misdirectional value of doing so."

"It evens out the playing field immediately," Harry agreed.

"Then I take the coins back," Pemberton continued. He held out his hand, but Sam was completely captivated by the coins.

"Are these yours?" Sam asked. He glanced up at Pemberton briefly and then returned his attention to the coins.

"They are. Actually, they were my late wife's," Pemberton stammered. "Is there something wrong with them?"

"On the contrary," Sam murmured. He focused on each coin, one at a time, squinting at first at the front and then the back. He held up one of the coins. "This one here is completely normal. Commonplace. It's in good shape, but nothing special."

He set that coin aside and then placed the other three half-dollars in a row in front of him on the table.

"These three," he continued. "These three are a completely different story."

* * *

WE WERE all seated around the table, listening closely as Sam outlined what made those three half-dollars something of interest.

"In 1964, Kennedy half-dollars were minted in Philadelphia. The first coins minted were the proof coins—which is like a test printing. A proof coin, which has a higher silver content, is of particular interest to collectors."

"Because of the higher silver content?" Harry asked.

"Yes, and because they're proof coins. They're rare. Or, at least, rarer," Sam explained. "There weren't a lot of proofs made of the Kennedy half-dollar."

"And that's what these are?" Pemberton said.

"Yes, but if I'm right—and I'm pretty sure I am—these are even more special," Sam said. He picked up one of the coins and looked at it closely. Almost lovingly.

"When they made a proof coin in Philadelphia, they didn't put any special mark on it. But when they minted a proof coin in Denver, they'd add a 'D' to the coin. See here?"

He slid the coin across the table and we all looked down. I wouldn't have noticed it if he hadn't pointed it out, but there was a small letter 'D' visible on the coin.

"All three of these coins are proof coins. And they all have the letter 'D,'" Sam explained.

"So, they were minted in Denver," Franny said. "And that makes them special?"

"No, there are plenty of Kennedy half-dollars which were minted in Denver. What makes these special is that Denver didn't mint <u>proof</u> coins. And they absolutely didn't mint proofs of the Kennedy half-dollar."

"So, are these fake?" Harry asked as he picked up the coin. I think he was as puzzled by Sam's dissertation as I was.

"No, I don't think so," Sam said slowly. "I think these might be the legendary three test coins that were minted in Denver before it was decided that Philadelphia would do the proofs on those coins."

"So, are you saying these coins are ... valuable?" Pemberton said hesitantly.

"I think valuable might be too weak a word." Sam pushed the coins across the table toward Pemberton.

"What are we talking?" Pemberton said tentatively. "Hundreds of dollars?"

"More, I think."

"Millions?

"No, probably not millions," Sam said. "But it's safe to say these three coins are worth thousands and thousands of dollars."

* * *

NEEDLESS TO SAY, that morning's lesson was immediately sidelined. Sam pulled out his phone to do a little research, checking a couple websites to verify his theory. And Pemberton huddled with Franny and Harry to discuss this sudden turn of events.

I sat in my chair, pondering the startling facts I had just heard. Despite a lack of evidence, I couldn't help but think that Pemberton's nightmares and the high worth of three of his coins must be linked in some way. Two such strange happenings had to be related, right?

Then I began to think about something Harry would have mentioned if the classes here at Lakeview Haven had been like his more traditional magic class.

If Harry had done his normal class, it would have involved more than just teaching the seniors one trick each. He would have talked about magic theory. And one of the ideas he would've touched on is the concept of the Before State and the After State.

That is, what was the situation <u>before</u> the trick? And what was the situation <u>after</u> the trick?

In order for a trick to be successful, the audience had to be keenly aware of how things were before the illusion ... and how things had changed after the illusion.

What disappeared? What transformed?

What change had occurred?

Harry was often heard saying to his students, including me, "If an audience can't answer those two questions—what was the Before State and what is now the After State—the trick will never make sense to them. Not ever."

So, I asked myself: in the case of Dr. Pemberton, what was the Before State? And what was the After State?

What had changed in the past few days, from Before to After?

Well, one answer was clear: he had learned a coin trick. A pretty good coin trick. In fact, a coin trick that he had demonstrated to just about <u>everyone</u> in his universe at Lakeview Haven.

As part of that trick, he let his audience members examine

the coins, to make sure they were real. In fact, he sort of <u>made</u> everyone look at the coins closely.

That was something which was different in his life—that was the change from the Before State to the After State.

He was doing a coin trick. And as part of that process, he was handing people coins and asking them to examine the coins closely.

And then he had terrifying nightmares.

And then he learned those coins were worth a fortune.

* * *

"You look very thoughtful, Eli," Harry said. His voice pulled me out of my reverie. "What's up?"

"I can't help but think there is some connection between the value of the coins and Dr. Pemberton's nightmares. Those are two big changes in his life in a very short time span. It would be weird if they <u>weren't</u> connected."

"But he didn't know the coins were valuable," Franny said. "None of us did, until Sam got here."

"But that doesn't mean someone else didn't know they were valuable," I said. "I mean, he showed them to a lot of people over the last few days."

"I showed them to <u>everyone</u>," Pemberton admitted.

"And if one of those people recognized how valuable the coins are, it isn't that big a leap for that same person to decide to break into his apartment to steal them."

"What? Dressed as Death?" Harry said.

"I don't know about that," I said. I turned to Pemberton. "You said it felt like Death was looking for something?"

"Yes. And I assumed it was me."

"But the coins weren't there," Harry said. "I had them in my apartment. For cleaning."

"But Death—or whoever it was—didn't know that," I said. "They just knew they had to get into Dr. Pemberton's apartment. To find the coins. And they couldn't let him know what they were doing. He couldn't be a reliable witness."

"So, they drugged him." This came from Franny.

"That would be a good way to do it," I agreed.

And then I thought about something else that had changed. A difference between the Before State and the After State.

It was a small thing, but that didn't mean it wasn't significant.

"Mikos the gardener says that the rabbits have been going after his favorite plants all of a sudden, out of the blue," I said. "Not all the plants; just the ones he calls his Lovely Ladies."

Franny narrowed her eyes. "What do they look like, these lovely ladies?"

I thought back to our initial tour of the grounds, when Mikos had first pointed them out to me.

"Tall plants with glossy leaves and deep red berries," I said.

"Belladonna," Franny said in a near whisper. "Which translates as Lovely Lady. Also known as Nightshade."

"But wait, isn't Belladonna poisonous?" Harry said.

"In the right dose, yes," Franny said. "Agatha Christie used it all the time in her stories. But she also had instances where the villain administered a smaller dose, which causes hallucinations."

"So, let me understand," Pemberton said. He'd perked up and begun to look sharper as this conversation had progressed. "Our working hypothesis is that a person or persons unknown sussed out the value of the coins I've been flashing around ... procured some Belladonna from the garden ... and somehow slipped me enough so that I've had serious and frightening hallucinations for two nights running? All in order to sneak into my apartment and steal—"

"More likely swap," Harry interjected.

"Yes, that makes sense," Pemberton agreed. "Swap out my very valuable coins for similar coins of far lesser value? That's our hypothesis?"

"That theory ticks a lot of boxes," Harry said.

"The problem is," Franny said as she leaned forward and focused on Pemberton. "You showed the coins to everyone and his brother around here. And everyone has access to the garden and the Belladonna plants. And I wouldn't be surprised if just about everyone knows you keep your French Doors propped open so Cerberus can let himself out when the need arises. So, our pool of suspects is huge. It's virtually everyone who has been in the building over the last three days."

"Yes, but it would have to be someone who not only knows me, but also knows Cerberus," Pemberton added. "Because, as you reported back to me, the dog didn't bark last night or the night before. Which means whoever entered my apartment was someone known to Cerberus."

I turned to Sam. "The dog only barks at strangers."

"Ah," he said.

"That's all true," Harry agreed. "But I think we can safely narrow it down to someone who works in the dining room. As that would put them in the best position to administer the drug to Pemberton. During one of the meals."

"That's swell," Franny said. "Except virtually everyone on the staff works in or around the kitchen at some point during the day."

"Other tasks as assigned," I said quietly.

"So that's still a considerable number of suspects," Harry said.

"However, we know something our perpetrator doesn't know," I offered.

"What's that?" Franny asked.

"We know what they're doing," I said. "And they don't know we know."

"That's true," Harry said. "So, all we need is a plan."

"That's all we need," I agreed. "And I think I have the beginnings of a decent one."

12

"Step one is that Dr. Pemberton needs to get out there and start doing his trick again," I said as I began to outline the plan; it was still incomplete, but it was coming to me in short bursts as I spoke to the small group. "And he should be sure to mention that Harry cleaned the coins and that they're now back in his possession."

"But I've shown it to virtually everyone," Pemberton lamented. "No one will want to see it again."

"Well then, we just have to teach you a new trick." I glanced at Harry and then at Sam. "And as luck would have it, you have two terrific teachers standing by."

"I think we can come up with something pretty quickly," Harry said.

"I already have an idea or two," Sam added.

"Fantastic." I turned back to Pemberton. "You'll need to focus on any staff member who might be in or around the kitchen and dining room during the course of their day. Every person you talk to has to walk away understanding two things: The coins were with Harry for the last two nights for cleaning. And they are now completely back in your possession."

"That's true," Harry said. "Our perpetrator probably won't make another attempt unless they know for sure they won't leave Pemberton's apartment empty-handed this time."

"Understood," Pemberton said.

In just a matter of minutes, my initial idea grew into a pretty neat three-step plan:

Step One: Make sure everyone in the universe of Lakeview Haven knew the Kennedy half-dollars were squarely back in Pemberton's possession.

Step Two: Give the perpetrator the opportunity to administer a dose of Belladonna to Pemberton (without actually letting the good doctor ingest the drug—Harry had some thoughts on how to do that).

Step Three: Catch the villain in the act of being villainous. (This part was still a bit sketchy in my mind.)

Once the plan was established, I'd like to say we wasted no time in putting it into motion. But considering the average age in the room was seventy-five, it's more accurate to say we slowly but steadily began executing our plan.

* * *

SAM DID INDEED HAVE some ideas for a new coin trick for Pemberton which would prominently feature the half-dollars.

"I think our best bet would be an Okito coin box," Sam suggested.

"That's ideal. It's quick to learn, it's portable, and it absolutely showcases the half-dollars," Harry agreed as he began to stand up. "Plus, I believe I have one back in the apartment."

Sam waved this away. "Save yourself a trip, Harry. What kind of coin magician would I be if I didn't always travel with an Okito coin box on me?"

He pulled the small, round brass container from his pocket. Picking up the coins, he demonstrated the trick for Pemberton.

He spread the coins out on the table, then placed them, one at a time, into the small container—it was just large enough to hold the four half-dollars snuggly. He put the brass cap on the container, placed it on the back of his closed fist, and then tapped the box.

As he did, he opened his fist. And the four coins dropped to the table, appearing to pass out of the box and right through his hand.

"Oh, that's lovely, Pemberton exclaimed.

"It's a classic," Sam said as he gathered up the coins again. "Now let me show you how it's done."

* * *

THE PROCESS of convincing the perpetrator that he or she was giving Pemberton a dose of Belladonna was a bit more involved. And something of a magic trick in itself.

Based on Franny's rough calculations, the Belladonna had probably been administered at some point during the evening meal. But to be on the safe side, they treated both lunch and dinner as potential threat situations, with lunch being something of a dress rehearsal.

Harry's plan was pretty straightforward: Franny would have lunch on her own; but instead of eating the food placed in front of her, she would secret it away into her purse: A sandwich (roast beef on rye), French fries, and (the trickiest part of all) a small side salad.

She pulled off the stunt like a pro, exiting the dining room with a purse stuffed with what would become Dr. Pemberton's lunch. She and Harry retired to their apartment; when he returned five minutes later, he was wearing a sport coat I hadn't seen in years.

"Can you believe I used to do my entire act with a live

chicken hidden inside this coat?" Harry whispered as we made our way back to the dining room.

"Plus, several decks of cards, a bottle of wine and one hundred sponge bunnies," I added.

"I just need to remember where everything is," Harry murmured as we headed down the hall. He patted the coat gently. "Sandwich here, fries there, and where did I put the salad?"

We stopped for a long moment until he'd located the salad portion of the meal. And then we continued on our way.

We met Pemberton just outside the dining room and the three of us went in, all doing our best to act completely natural.

We made certain that each person ordered a different dish (with Pemberton picking the same meal as Franny had) and then waited eagerly for the food to arrive.

Once the three meals were in front of us, our lunch became something of a well-orchestrated dance: I would reach for the salt, to cover Harry's snatching Pemberton's sandwich and swapping it for the one in his coat. Pemberton would reach for the water pitcher, which allowed me to grab the fries off his plate, while Harry swapped in the ones Franny had given him.

The salad was the trickiest part, but we got lucky: Across the room, someone dropped some plates, creating a loud and startling racket. Sensing this was the perfect time, I reached over and simply grabbed Pemberton's salad, scooping it up in my fist. An instant later, Harry deposited a handful of salad in the same spot. The suspect salad went into the napkin on my lap, which I folded and snuck into my coat pocket.

Pemberton, looking completely innocent, then began to cheerfully chomp on his salad.

To anyone who might have been observing our table, the illusion that Pemberton had eaten the meal placed in front of him was stunningly real.

"That was a good rehearsal, gentlemen," Harry said quietly

as we left the dining room. "If we can pull it off again tonight, the trap will be well set."

"I agree," Pemberton said, echoing Harry's low volume. "Just make sure that Franny does one key thing."

"What's that?"

"Tell her not to order the soup."

* * *

THROUGHOUT THE DAY, Pemberton did his best to put his new coin trick in front of anyone who would stand still long enough to watch it. And for those who couldn't spare the time, he would keep pace with them as they walked along, executing the trick while on the move. He even incorporated some patter of his own ("You see, once you clean the dirt off the coins, they more easily can pass through solid matter"), which helped reinforce the idea of where the coins had been for the past two nights.

"I'll say this much for your plan, Eli," Dr. Pemberton said that evening. "Nothing improves a magic trick more than doing it repeatedly for several hours in front of a variety of audiences. I wouldn't call myself a pro by any standard of that definition, but I will say this much: I'm actually not bad at executing the Okito coin box trick."

We were seated, as we had been on the first night, in the library. The port had been brought out, but we were only pretending to sip at it. We all realized the next few hours would require nothing less than clear and focused thinking.

"I agree," I said. "You've got it down. Once this is all settled, we'll get you a restaurant gig and you'll become a pro in no time flat."

Harry, who had been listening impatiently, interjected. "Yes, yes, yes. So, what is the final phase of your plan, Eli," he said, keeping his voice low. "How do we proceed?"

"I've come up with about twenty really elaborate traps, but I think the simplest plan would be the best," I said.

"Always a good idea," Harry agreed.

"Here's what I'm proposing. As we did on the first night, you and I will accompany a supposedly tipsy Dr. Pemberton to his apartment. Once he's safely inside, we'll both retire to your apartment, under the pretense that I'm too inebriated to drive.

"That's the picture we'll present to the world at large here at Lakeview Haven," I continued. "But once we're in our respective apartments, I will sneak through the back garden and slip into Dr. Pemberton's apartment, unseen by our burglar."

"Through the always open French Doors," Pemberton added.

"Exactly," I said. "At the same time, Dr. Pemberton will cover that same ground in reverse, taking refuge in your apartment next door. Completely out of harm's way."

"Much appreciated," Pemberton said.

"Meanwhile," I continued. "I will hide out in the living room. And I'll wait for our perpetrator to make his or her entrance. And when they do—bingo—we'll have them. Red-handed. Whatever that means."

"The term originated in Scotland during the 15th century," Pemberton explained. "It was initially used to describe apprehending someone for a homicide, when they still had fresh blood on their hands. Hence, red-handed."

"Well, we'll have no blood on anyone's hands tonight," Harry said firmly. "I'm not liking the idea of you alone in the apartment with this perpetrator."

"I won't be alone," I said, trying to sound as reassuring as I could. "Cerberus will be with me. And I'll also have this."

I held up my iPhone.

"As soon as anything starts to happen, I'll hit the video record button. That will be our proof."

"Good thought," Harry said. "Otherwise, this could easily

turn into a 'your word against their word' sort of situation. At the very least, the video will prove they illegally entered Pemberton's apartment."

"It's an excellent strategy, Eli," Pemberton said. "I'd suggest we drink to it, but that would go against the plan as stated."

"Well, we can toast and pretend to drink," Harry suggested.

We each held up our glasses and clinked them.

"To the plan," Pemberton said.

"To the plan," Harry echoed.

We then all pretended to sip the port.

Considering how things ultimately turned out, a couple of drinks probably wouldn't have changed the outcome significantly.

Either way, I'd still end up unconscious on the floor.

13

The apartment swap was not nearly as dramatic as a Soviet-era prisoner exchange; at the appointed time, Pemberton and I simply passed each other in the garden. We nodded at one another silently. And then he disappeared into Harry and Franny's apartment, and I ducked into his.

The entire exchange took maybe ten seconds and—as far as I could see—went completely unobserved.

And, of course, because Cerberus knew me, he didn't make a peep when I entered the dark apartment. I gave him a welcoming pat on the head, and he rewarded me with a friendly wag of his tail. And then he went and lay down in front of the couch, settling into his oversized dog bed. In just a few moments, he was quietly snoring.

Sleep, of course, was not an option for me.

The dim light in the room came via the moon, which offered a shadowy view of the French Doors and the garden beyond.

I flipped on the flashlight on my phone and scanned the room. It all looked as it had the first night Harry and I'd rushed in, responding to Pemberton's screams.

The four half-dollars sat with the rest of the doctor's pocket change on the kitchen counter, suggesting he had simply emptied his pockets before heading to bed. Which was the impression we'd wanted to give our potential intruder.

I made one small adjustment to the pile and then flipped off the phone's flashlight. To an outside observer, it was supposed to look like Pemberton was in bed. I needed to maintain that illusion.

I found a reasonably comfortable chair and positioned it so that I could see the French Doors, but in such a way that someone entering wouldn't immediately see me.

I still had my phone out; I clicked on the camera app, chose the video option, and settled into the chair. I was ready to go.

On the two previous occasions—if our premise was correct—the burglar had waited about an hour to make sure Pemberton was in bed and in the full thrall of the Belladonna.

So, I figured I had a few minutes before anything significant was going to happen.

As it does, my mind began to wander. And so—of course—I started to second-guess this alleged plan I'd cobbled together.

I sometimes think my greatest skill is self-doubt. It certainly finds a way to take the lead in most situations. If I could monetize uncertainty, I'd be a rich man.

My mind was suddenly flooded with unhelpful thoughts.

What if I was wrong about one or more details in this scenario? What if Pemberton wasn't being drugged? What if he was just on this side of being crazy? What if no one has been sneaking into the apartment? What if he really had been hallucinating?

Well, so what? No harm, no foul, I thought, trying to push those intrusive thoughts out of view.

The worst that might happen if he hadn't been drugged was that Pemberton would have his nightly freak-out next door, under the watchful eyes of Franny and Harry. And if that occurred, we'd know for sure it wasn't the Belladonna. I may have been doubtful about some parts of this plan, but I was pretty sure we'd kept Pemberton from being drugged by persons unknown.

So, even if my plan didn't reveal the identity of an alleged burglar, at the very least it would confirm—or throw into serious doubt—the sanity of Dr. Pemberton.

The more I thought about it, the more any result could be positioned as a win-win: we'd end up with a positive outcome, regardless of whether there was an actual burglary or not.

While I was congratulating myself on successfully squelching my ever-present insecurity, what I didn't realize was that there was a flaw in my plan.

And it was absolutely my fault.

I had made a presumption.

And I knew presumptions were bad things, if only because of the number of times Harry had said to me: "You know, Eli, when you presume, you make a prez out of you and me."

Of course, we both knew he meant 'assume,' not 'presume.' But he didn't care. Harry loves to tell jokes wrong, just to get a rise out of people.

When I was a teenager, Harry delighted in taking a classic joke ("How do you get down from an elephant? You don't, you get down from a duck.") and tell it thusly: "How to you climb off an elephant? You don't, you climb off a duck."

The mystified expressions on my friends' faces would delight Harry for days on end.

Anyway, at the very moment when it was actually too late to do anything about it, I realized I had made a presumption: I presumed—because Pemberton famously always left his French Doors ajar—that our villain was going to use that as their point of entry into the dark apartment.

What I had failed to take into account was—given our hypothesis that the perpetrator was a member of the staff—it would be just as easy (if not easier) to use their pass key to enter the apartment via the front door.

I should have thought it through: That point of access was far less suspicious than creeping through the garden in the middle of the night.

But, as I mentioned, I hadn't considered this possibility until it was too late.

And, of course, Cerberus was no help whatsoever. He may have heard someone come in the front door, but since he immediately realized it wasn't a stranger, he didn't make a peep. In fact, given this was the third such occurrence for this late-night entrance, he may have added it to his list of "things humans do." And so he wasn't giving it a second thought.

While I think he's a terrific dog, a little warning from him would have been appreciated.

I simply didn't count on the burglar coming down the main hall, and through the front door. No one would think twice seeing a staff member walking down the hall at any time of day.

And all the staff had access to pass keys, because the mantra at Lakeview was: *Other tasks as assigned.*

So, while I was keeping an eye on the French doors, our burglar walked right in the front door with a master key.

I can't speak to their exact actions, but I can recount the impact they had on me.

They hit me. On the head. With something very heavy and likely very blunt.

That was the last thing I remembered until I woke up on the floor with Harry, Franny and Dr. Pemberton standing over me.

* * *

"Eli, don't worry, we're calling an ambulance," Harry said, his face a map of worry and concern.

I sat up very slowly.

"I don't think you need to bother." I tentatively touched the back of my head. I felt a very familiar bump in an equally familiar spot. "Whoever it was, they hit me in the same spot where I always get hit. It's like there's a bullseye on the back of my head."

I sat up even further, testing the limits of what my body was going to allow me to do. It felt bad, but not terrible. Certainly not life-threatening.

"The coins!" Pemberton barked. "They got the coins!"

"No," I said as I began to shake my head and immediately realized that was a terrible idea. "They got <u>some</u> coins, but not <u>the</u> coins."

I slowly and painfully reached into my pocket and pulled out Pemberton's clean and shiny Kennedy half-dollars.

"It occurred to me that there was every chance in the world our burglar might flummox our well-oiled plan," I said. "So, I swapped them out with four regular half-dollars."

"But at some point they're going to realize they have the wrong coins," Harry said.

"They've probably figured it out already," Franny said. "And I'm sure they're not happy about it."

Pemberton rubbed his hands together nervously. "Do you think they'll come back tonight? Make another attempt?"

I wanted to shake my head in response, but every fiber of my being told me not to attempt it. "Given that they found me here rather than you, I would guess they realize we're on to them. So, it seems unlikely they'll come back tonight. Or maybe ever."

"And it also seems unlikely that we will ever know who it was," Harry said.

"Oh, I'll be able to tell you exactly who it was," I said.

It felt like I was ready to stand up and I made the attempt.

With the help of Harry and Pemberton, I successfully got to my feet.

"You know who it was?" Franny said. "You saw them?"

"No, I didn't see a thing," I admitted. "But I should have no trouble pointing them out in a crowd. Assuming it's dark like it was in here when they whacked me upside the head and stole the coins."

They may have thought I was kidding, but I wasn't. I knew I could easily and accurately identify my assailant.

But first I had to make a phone call.

14

"To be honest, Eli, a situation like this is a little below my pay grade. I haven't worked a small burglary case in a number of years."

"I'm sure it will all come back to you."

Detective Randolph made a sound that was impossible to decipher, but it sounded positive. It seemed like he was still willing to help me out.

Glenn Randolph was with the Minneapolis Police Department, working primarily in the Robbery and Financial Crimes Division. This usually meant larger-scale offenses, often involving white collar criminals and millions and millions of dollars.

Randolph, and a handful of his law enforcement pals, were also regulars at the bar next to Chicago Magic, which is where I'd met him.

He had the look of a retired wrestler, and with good reason. He'd been a national contender during his college days. Even though time had taken its toll on him, he still had moments where he moved with the elegance of a top-level athlete.

I wouldn't exactly call us friends, but I had offered helpful advice on a case or two, which had turned out well for him. So, Detective Randolph was the first person I considered contacting for this final chapter of the Pemberton coins case.

He stood alongside me as staff members filled into the Lakeview Haven Activities Room.

Randolph had made the request for the gathering directly to the management and they quickly complied. I think they wanted to avoid any PR fallout if it became public knowledge that someone was burglarizing residents' apartments.

Perhaps drugging them.

And also assaulting me. Although I think they cared less about this last point than the other issues.

Franny and Harry stood in the back of the room, on either side of Dr. Pemberton. He had managed to sleep soundly the previous night without any nightmares or hallucinations. This provided further evidence that someone had been administering drugs to him.

I recognized most of the faces in the room: Samantha, who had taken us on the first tour of Lakeview Haven. Big Steve, who was in charge of the concierge staff. Chef Anton, who oversaw the kitchen staff. Ruby, the supervisor of the cleaning crew. Claire, who was the program director and also produced the weekly podcast. Even Mikos the gardener and Cornelius, the President of the Resident Board, had been called in for this impromptu staff meeting.

"So, who's your prime suspect?" Randolph asked quietly.

"I really don't have one," I admitted.

And it was true; I could make a case against any one of the staff members. They all had, as the saying goes, means, motive and opportunity.

Of all of them, Claire was the only one where I'd been present when Pemberton had her examine the coins. At the time, I didn't know there was anything special about the half-dollars. And, as far as I could remember, Claire's reaction hadn't suggested she recognized anything exceptional about them either. Although she had casually mentioned that her father was a coin collector. But, then as now, I didn't know if that was significant or not.

As for the other folks? I hadn't been around when Pemberton asked them to take a look at the half-dollars before launching into his coin routine. So, I had no idea if any one of them had offered up any sort of reaction when they recognized the value of those coins.

In short, I didn't know who had committed the crimes. But I was pretty sure that—whoever that person might be—they were currently standing in front of me in the Activities Room at Lakeview Haven.

Once he had verified everyone was there, Detective Randolph launched into a short presentation. I had outlined it for him, but like any pro, he'd inserted some tweaks and made it his own.

"Good morning, everyone," Randolph said. "Thank you for joining us. I know you're all anxious to get to work this morning, so we'll get through this as quickly as we can."

He paused as he scanned the room, and then he gestured toward me. "As some of you may have heard, there was a burglary of one of the resident's apartments last night in which a guest—Eli Marks here—was assaulted. In addition to the assault, some coins were stolen. Coins which, as I'm sure the assailant is now well aware, are close to worthless."

"This is outrageous," Cornelius said, nearly shouting. "If we aren't safe in our apartments, then where are we supposed to be safe? I intend to take this up before the full Board in an emergency meeting tonight."

His outburst created its own hubbub throughout the room. Detective Randolph waited for the murmuring to dissipate before continuing.

"That's fine," he said. "However, our purpose this morning is to identify the burglar, who apparently entered the apartment with a pass key. Which narrows the scope of our investigation to only the staff here at Lakeview Haven."

"So, I'm not a suspect?" Cornelius said, his eyes narrowing.

"That remains to be seen."

This produced another group murmur. This time, Randolph didn't wait for it to die down.

"To simplify things, let me ask this: Would the person who entered Dr. Pemberton's apartment last night please step forward?"

This was such an outrageous request that it immediately silenced the room. Employees looked around, curious to see if anyone was going to take responsibility for the crime.

"No takers?" Randolph said. "Well, it was worth a shot. Let's go with Plan B."

That was a cue and Franny and Harry were right on top of it. Harry flipped a switch by the door and the electric shutters rolled into place, quickly covering the windows in the room.

At the same time, Franny turned to the switch plate on the wall next to her and flipped switch after switch, until all the lights in the room were out.

With the windows covered and the lights out, the room got dark quickly. Because the door was open, it didn't get pitch black, but it was certainly dark enough for my purposes.

"I would ask that everyone in here please raise your hands. Both hands, please," Randolph commanded.

This odd request was met with obvious skepticism, but one after another, employees throughout the room began to raise their hands.

While they did that, I flipped an app on my phone into "on" mode, which switched the light on my iPhone flashlight to UV.

I began to address the room.

"Although the coins which were taken last night were not the valuable half-dollars our thief was looking for, they each did have something special about them," I said. "Namely, each coin was coated with a dusting of a phosphorous powder. It's not visible to the eye, but it absolutely comes to life under UV light."

I slowly made my way through the room, scanning the light across all the raised hands.

Past Claire, past Samantha, past Big Steve, past Ruby, past Mikos.

"My hands are a bit dirty, sorry," Mikos said. "I was digging."

"Not a problem, Mikos."

I continued to scan the employees' hands and was starting to panic. Just a little bit. But it was growing.

If this didn't work, I didn't have a backup plan.

There was no Plan C or any of the twenty-three letters after it.

If this idea failed, I had nothing.

And then I got to Chef Anton. His arms were folded, his hands deeply buried and out of sight. He scowled at me, his mustache twitching in what felt like a threatening manner.

"This is a violation of my civil rights," he said slowly.

"Actually, it's not," Detective Randolph said. "But if you don't want to put your hands out now—voluntarily—we'll just do the same scan once we have you in handcuffs. Which I am more than happy to do."

It had been a while since I'd seen two alpha males square off like this. It was sort of fun.

I think Chef Anton realized he wasn't going to win this round. He slowly—oh, so slowly—pulled his hands from under his arms. I could tell he was attempting to wipe his fingers against the fabric of his chef's tunic, in the mad hope that it would whisk away any of the pesky phosphorous.

No such luck.

As Nathan had lamented when he first demonstrated the

card trick which employed the phosphorous and the UV light, the powder was a bear to remove.

This point was driven home when the UV light on my iPhone landed on the chef's long fingers.

They glowed blue. It was subdued, but it was unassailable.

"Do you have any explanation for this?" Randolph asked.

"I was making a blueberry pie," Chef Anton hissed through gritted teeth. Even he was having trouble selling this alibi.

"Too bad you won't have a chance to sample it," Randolph said as he pulled out a pair of handcuffs.

This must have been a signal to two uniformed officers, who had been waiting patiently outside the room. They stepped in, signaling to Chef Anton that if he was going to make a fuss, they had the manpower to handle it.

He was handcuffed and out of the room in record time, with Randolph still reading him his Miranda rights as they walked out the door.

As the angry chef passed Harry, Franny and Pemberton, the two older men were rolling half-dollars across the backs of their fingers. It's a slick coin manipulation which has no real value except that it looks pretty cool. Which, in magic, is often enough.

Harry, of course, was manipulating the coin like the pro he is. But Pemberton's version wasn't half bad; he was clearly new to the technique, but he put on a good show.

Both of the old guys grinned at Chef Anton as he was taken away, flashing the half-dollars in a sort of silent, mocking gesture.

For his part, Anton didn't seem particularly impressed by the moves.

He simply growled as the two cops led him down the hall.

15

"That was a heckuva show."

This self-praising pronouncement came from Cornelius, but his words were echoed by many of the people exiting the room. The crowd consisted of a mix of Lakeview Haven residents and staff members, all abuzz after the entertaining performance they had just witnessed.

It was three days later, and the students in Harry's magic class had put on a short magic display for the residents. The Activities Room had been packed to capacity, with every seat filled and several latecomers left standing in the back.

And all the students had done a wonderful job with their acts. Well, most of them at least.

Irma had kicked off the show with her polished version of the Self-Coloring Coloring Book. She'd come up with some sweet, grandma-style jokes about spoiling her grandkids, which got big laughs of recognition from the audience. And she executed the magic flawlessly, with nimble fingers that deftly handled the oversized prop.

This lively opening act was followed by Cornelius and his painful attempt at the Linking Rings. As a politician, retired or otherwise, one would have expected him to have strong presentation skills. However, he had zero ability to read the room or engage the crowd. Any energy produced by Irma's act was promptly sucked out of the room by Cornelius' clumsy performance. His rings clanged together loudly, and he dropped them several times, scrambling to pick them up as the audience looked on awkwardly. But he beamed throughout and although he exited to light applause, he acted like it was a standing ovation.

Luckily, Harry—being a seasoned performer—had strategically positioned Cornelius between two strong acts. This brilliant bit of show structuring paid off.

By the time Fatima was thirty-seconds into her delightful version of the Miser's Dream, the audience had already forgotten about Cornelius' dismal showing. Fatima's lively patter entranced the crowd as she told a clever and funny story about making change for a genie at her bank. And her smooth handling of the coins and bucket demonstrated a mastery of the illusion far beyond her beginner status.

Next, Lisbeth pulled a willing volunteer, Mikos the gardener, out of the audience for her creative sponge ball routine. I'd tracked down some cute sponge bunnies and she'd tailored her act around Mikos' garden being humorously overrun by the fuzzy creatures.

Mikos played along perfectly, eliciting laughs from the delighted crowd. As he left the makeshift stage, he proclaimed, "Those rabbits, they bother me no more!" Which was absolutely true, since the culprit who had been ravaging his beloved Belladonna plants was now safely behind bars.

The final act of the evening was a touching tribute by Dr. Pemberton. When it came time to pick an illusion for the show, he and Harry determined that his Sympathetic Coins routine was too intimate for such a large venue. Plus, just about everyone present had already seen it performed up close and personal at least once.

Instead, Pemberton decided to honor his late friend Martin's memory by learning and masterfully executing The Professor's Nightmare routine.

His handling of the three ropes was a simple yet lovely tribute, and the perfect bittersweet conclusion to the show. More than a few audience members dabbed at their eyes as Pemberton took his bow. And I'm proud to admit that I was one of them.

* * *

As the crowd filtered out of the room, still abuzz from the evening's entertainment, Claire approached Harry with an eager smile.

"The magic show was a huge hit," she exclaimed. "People are already asking about the next class and when you'll be doing this again."

Harry grinned at the enthusiastic young woman. "I'm glad folks enjoyed it. I'm certainly not opposed to teaching another round. But now that Franny and I are fully settled in at Lakeview—and free from homeowner headaches—we've decided to do some traveling for pleasure, not work."

"Yes, we have a long list of places we want to finally see," Franny eagerly added.

"However, if you want to get a new class going right away in my absence, I'm sure my nephew Eli here would be happy to take over the teaching duties."

He turned to me expectantly. "What do you say, Eli? Ready to step up from teaching assistant to full professor? Are you willing to handle the next session without me?"

"Sure, sounds like fun," I responded automatically, without really thinking it through.

When will I ever learn to think things through before committing? Probably never, if past history is any indication.

"That's fantastic news!" Claire exclaimed, clearly excited at the prospect. "I already have a few eager students signed up and raring to go."

"Wonderful. Thanks again for stepping in, Eli," Harry said, clapping me on the back. He and Franny then headed toward the door.

"No problem at all!" Then I turned back to Claire with a smile. "You said some students have already signed up?"

"Yes indeed," she replied, gesturing behind me with a knowing look. "And I believe you're already acquainted with this trio."

I spun around, and sure enough, there stood the Spring Sisters, staring severely at me with their trademark ominous expressions.

The one in the middle rasped, "We're no longer just auditing." Her two cohorts nodded along creepily.

I gulped hard, quickly scanning the room for any sight of my uncle.

But Harry had just flawlessly pulled off one of the greatest illusions of his storied career.

He had completely and utterly vanished.

READ DR. PEMBERTON'S BOOK

IT'S MY FIRST TIME GETTING OLD (SO EXCUSE ME IF I GO ASTRAY)

Remember the book Dr. Pemberton talked about writing in "The Professor's Nightmare"? His philosophical treatise on aging?

Well, even though he's fictional, he did find time to write it!

Aging: The Adventure You Didn't Know You Signed Up For.
Embark on a profound exploration of life, aging, and the mysteries beyond with "It's My First Time Getting Old (So

Excuse Me If I Go Astray)". This unique work of fiction masterfully weaves philosophical thought with an intimate journey into the realities of aging and mortality.

The book presents the intellectual musings of the fictional Dr. Charles Pemberton. As a philosopher at the brink of his eighth decade, Dr. Pemberton brings a wealth of wisdom, personal experiences, and eclectic pop culture references to his narrative, creating a resonant exploration of the universal human experience.

Click HERE to Grab Your Free Copy!

Or go to: https://BookHip.com/TVVHFDQ

GET YOUR FREE ELI MARKS SHORT STORY BUNDLE

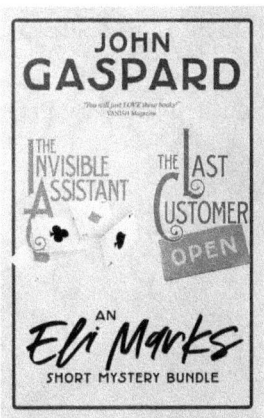

The Eli Marks Short Mystery Bundle
"The Invisible Assistant" & "The Last Customer"
Two short-story cozy mysteries in one!

"You will just LOVE these books."– VANISH Magazine

The Invisible Assistant
There's no question it was murder. But who killed whom?

What begins as a typical corporate event for magician Eli Marks turns into a twisted mystery when he is called to the site of a recent murder/suicide. Confronted by the details of the grisly crime scene, Eli must sort through the post-mortem clues - and the bickering of the officials as well as a poorly-timed allergy attack - to determine just who murdered whom.

The Last Customer

The request was a first for Eli Marks: "Can you help me make my tuba disappear?"

Magician (and magic shop owner) Eli Marks is confronted with this odd demand just before he is about to close up shop for the day. Over the next few tense minutes, he finds a solution to that question which also, fortunately, puts him the positive side of what turns out to be a life-or-death situation.

Click HERE to grab your free copy!

Or go to www.elimarksmysteries.com

GET YOUR FREE COMO LAKE PLAYERS SHORT MYSTERY

An Opening Nightmare

A Como Lake Players Short Mystery

A Killer Show, With the Corpses To Prove It

When an audience member is stabbed in the middle of an Opening Night performance, Leah must figure out who this clever killer is ... and make sure they don't kill the run of her show! Or murder her, as well!

A great introduction to The Como Lake Players mystery series: New Executive Director (and former actress) Leah Sexton must navigate the twisty world of community theater while dealing with crazy Board members, egomaniacal directors, self-centered actors ... and the occasional cold-blooded killer.

"This new cozy series will keep you guessing until the very end!" — Storeybook Reviews

Go to: https://www.albertsbridgebooks.com/

LISTEN TO THE PODCAST

Listen to the audiobook versions of the Eli Marks mysteries ... for FREE. And learn more about the lives of magicians and performers and other ideas found in the Eli Marks series.

Click HERE to listen!

Each episode includes interviews with guest experts and magicians ... plus a reading of a chapter from an Eli Marks mystery. Season One presents great guests (like Dick Cavett and The Amazing Kreskin) and a full reading of the first book in the series, "The Ambitious Card."

Season Two provides a free reading of the second book in the series, "The Bullet Catch," plus great interviews.

Click HERE to listen!

Or go to www.elimarksmysteries.com

JOIN THE NEWSLETTER

Keep in touch about all the books at Albert's Bridge books —
The Como Lake Players mysteries ... the Eli Marks mysteries ...
plus occasional deals on other mysteries! And no spam!

Click HERE to join!

Or go to www.elimarksmysteries.com

BOOKS BY JOHN GASPARD

Stand-Alone Novels
THE SWORD & MR. STONE
A CHRISTMAS CARL
THE GREYHOUND OF THE BASKERVILLES
THE GREYHOUND & GATSBY
A GREYHOUND INVESTIGATES THE MYSTERIOUS
AFFAIR AT STYLES
THE RIPPEROLOGISTS

Filmmaking/Writing Books
THE POPCORN PRINCIPLES
MORE POPCORN PRINCIPLES: THE SEQUEL!
FAST, CHEAP AND UNDER CONTROL
FAST, CHEAP AND WRITTEN THAT WAY
TELL THEM IT'S A DREAM SEQUENCE
WOMEN MAKE MOVIES

ABOUT THE AUTHOR

John is author of the Eli Marks mystery series as well as four other stand-alone novels, *"The Sword & Mr. Stone," "A Christmas Carl," "The Greyhound of the Baskervilles"* and *"The Ripperologists."*

He also writes the *Como Lake Players* mystery series.

In real life, John's not a magician, but he has directed six low-budget features that cost very little and made even less—that's no small trick.

He's also written books on the subject of low-budget film-making. Ironically, they've made more than the films. Those books *("Fast, Cheap and Under Control"* and *"Fast, Cheap and Written That Way")* are available in eBook, Paperback and audiobook formats.

John lives in Minnesota and shares his home with his lovely wife, several dogs, a few cats and a handful of pet allergies.

Find out more at: https://www.albertsbridgebooks.com and https://www.elimarksmysteries.com.

facebook.com/JohnGaspardAuthorPage

x.com/johngaspard

instagram.com/johngaspard

bookbub.com/authors/john-gaspard